Introducing
Philosophy of Religion

Dilwyn Hunt

Nelson Thornes

Published in 2005 by:
Nelson Thornes Ltd
Delta Place
27 Bath Road
CHELTENHAM
GL53 7TH
United Kingdom

08 09 / 10 9 8 7 6 5 4

A catalogue record for this book is available from the British Library

ISBN 978-0-7487-9466-9

Illustrations by Ian West, Steve Ballinger and Angela Lumley
Page make-up by Pantek Arts Ltd, Maidstone, Kent

Printed and bound in China

Contents

Rock 'n' roll! What's that above my head Mrs Grosvenor? Are we doing philossopy?
Philosophy, Matthew. The word is philosophy. Believe me, this is an adventure for both of us.

Time chart

This time chart shows when some of the people mentioned in this book lived.

BCE/CE 0	
	Death of Jesus 30 AD
100	Irenaeus 130–202
	Plotinus 205–70
200	
300	Augustine 354–430
400	Attila the Hun attacks Rome 455
500	Birth of Muhammad 570
600	Monks from Iona teach Christianity in Northumbria 633
700	The Vikings invade Europe 780
	Charlemagne crowned Emperor of the Romans 800
800	
900	The Abbey of Cluny founded 910
1000	

1000	Battle of Hastings 1066
1100	Francis of Assisi 1182–1226
1200	Thomas Aquinas 1225–74
1300	Beginning of the Hundred Years War with France 1337
	The Black Death plague breaks out in Europe 1361
1400	Joan of Arc is burnt at the stake 1431
	Christopher Columbus discovers the New World 1492
1500	Francis Bacon 1561–1626
1600	Benedict Spinoza 1632–77
	Isaac Newton's theory of gravitation 1687
1700	Joseph Butler 1692–1752 David Hume 1711–76 Thomas Paine 1737–1809 William Paley 1743–1805 Friedrich Schleiermacher 1768–1834
1800	John Henry Newman 1801–90 John Stuart Mill 1806–73 Charles Darwin 1809–82 William James 1842–1910
	Bertrand Russell 1872–1970
1900	John Wisdom 1904–93 John Hick b. 1922 Richard Swinburne b. 1934 Man lands on the moon 1969
2000	

Introduction

What is philosophy of religion?

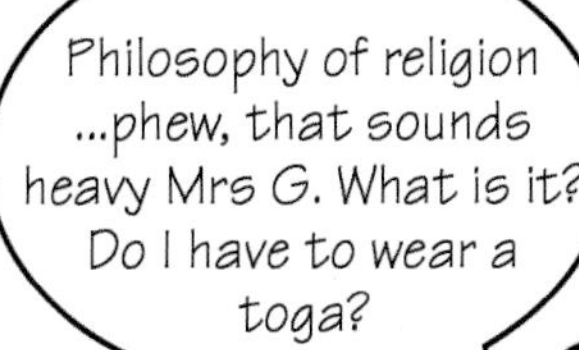

This book is about religion. That should be no surprise given its title. However, this book is not about religious festivals, holy books, churches, mosques or places of pilgrimage. It is not about ceremonies like baptism, arti or communion. All those aspects of religion are very important. But they are not what this book is about.

This book is about ideas and beliefs. It is about what religions claim about the world we live in. Of course, there are many religions in the world and they are not all the same. Nevertheless, many religions share some beliefs and make similar claims. Here are a few of the claims made by some important religions today:

- there is a God
- God made the universe
- when we die, death is not the end
- miracles really do happen.

Many of these claims made by religions are claims about the world as it is today. They are called 'truth-claims'. Truth-claims can be scrutinised and examined. It is possible to look rigorously at a truth-claim and ask questions such as:

- is there good evidence to back up this truth-claim?
- is this evidence convincing?
- what reasons are used to support this truth-claim?
- are these reasons logical?

Scrutinising religious truth-claims in this way is called 'philosophy of religion'. Philosophy is not just for the super brainy. Anybody can do philosophy.

The cosmological argument

Is there a God? All around the world billions of people believe in a God. But what is God? We could get bogged down trying to answer this question. Let us try and answer it by saying that God is the living, Supreme Being that created the universe. This is not a perfect definition of God, but it is enough to get us started. Is there any evidence that this Supreme Being really exists?

Over the years, many people have tried to argue that there is a God. St Thomas Aquinas put one of the most famous of these arguments forward. Thomas Aquinas' argument is called the **cosmological argument**. Aquinas was a Christian friar who lived about 800 years ago. His argument goes roughly like this:

The cosmological argument

Look at the world around you and you will see the sun, the moon and the planets. The whole universe contains millions of stars. The sun rises and falls every day. The moon circles around the Earth. Every day the tide comes in and goes out. Every year the seasons come and go. How did this vast universe get here? How did it all get started? What was it that kicked it all off and made it in the first place? What set everything in motion?

Things do not just come out of nothing. Things do not just move on their own. Something must have set the world in motion and made it in the first place. The whole vast cosmos turning and moving through space did not just happen. Something made it all happen. That something was God. Because there is a universe, there has to be a God that made that universe. Therefore there is a God.

Thomas Aquinas (c.1225–74)
Aquinas argued that 'nothing comes from nothing' or, as he wrote in Latin, *ex nihilo, nihil fit*.

In the universe there are, at scientists' last estimate, 100 billion galaxies, billions of stars, solar systems, and planets – all moving through space. How did it all come about? What caused it all to happen?

Using an analogy

One way to make an argument clearer is by using an **analogy**. An analogy is when you suggest a likeness to something else. For example, it is sometimes argued that space exploration will bring lots of benefits to humankind in the same way that exploration by people like Christopher Columbus also bought benefits to humankind. Using an analogy is sometimes called 'reasoning from a parallel case'.

Below is an example of using an analogy. The domino analogy is an attempt to make the cosmological argument clearer and more vivid. Is it a true analogy? Is the analogy flawed in any way?

The domino analogy

The cosmological argument is like a row of dominoes when one is pushed over. Imagine you had thousands of dominoes. In a big room you placed each domino on its edge so that if one domino fell it would knock another domino over, and that in turn would knock another domino over, and so on. You could leave the dominoes for a day, a week, or even years, and unless something happened like an earthquake or a mouse scampered past and knocked over a domino, nothing would happen. The first domino would not spontaneously fall over on its own. The first domino could not knock itself over setting off a chain reaction causing all the other dominoes to fall. Things do not just happen unless something causes them to happen.

Suppose one day you walked into your big room just at the moment when the dominoes were halfway through falling over. You look back along the line of fallen dominoes and you can see that the first domino has fallen, causing the others to fall. Naturally, you would ask, 'What caused the first domino to fall?' What was the energy, the force, the cause, or the being that started it all?

The cosmological argument is similar to the situation with the dominoes. If the first domino did not spontaneously fall over, we would be right to think something caused it to fall. In a similar way, unless the universe suddenly decided to start, it is reasonable for us to think that before the universe began there was something that began it all. The cosmological argument says that that something was God.

We know a lot more today about the universe than Aquinas did eight hundred years ago. Particularly associated with the ideas of the Belgian astrophysicist Georges Lemaître (1894–1966), the idea of the **Big Bang** is now accepted by most scientists today. It goes like this:

The Big Bang

The scientific evidence tells us that about 14 billion years ago the universe was an enormously dense nucleus. An incredibly powerful explosion occurs, a Big Bang. Within a millionth of a second after the explosion protons, neutrons and electrons are created.

In the explosion enormous heat is generated, but as the universe cools down a little, elements like helium and hydrogen are created. From these elements stars, galaxies, planets and solar systems are formed. As the universe continues to cool, on at least one planet (which we call Earth), about 3 billion years ago, life begins to develop.

Where did the dense nucleus come from?

The Big Bang theory starts with the idea that the universe was an enormously dense nucleus and that this nucleus exploded. The theory really tells us what happened after this explosion. What the theory does not tell us is how the nucleus got there in the first place. Also, the theory does not make it very clear what made the nucleus explode. Therefore, on the basis of Aquinas' principle that nothing comes from nothing, it is reasonable to say, 'There must have been something that made the nucleus. There must be something that made it explode. That something was God.'

The Pulsating Universe

A more recent development of the Big Bang theory is the idea of the Pulsating Universe. This idea was first suggested by the American cosmologist Allan Sandage. The Pulsating Universe theory claims that after the Big Bang, the universe expands outwards but eventually it stops expanding. It then starts to implode back on itself. Everything gets sucked back into a dense nucleus, which then explodes, starting the whole cycle off again. The cycle of Big Bang, expansion, contraction and Big Bang again just keeps going on and on.

Does this idea of the Pulsating Universe make any difference to Aquinas' cosmological argument? If there is a dense nucleus which is constantly exploding, expanding and then contracting, is it not reasonable to ask, 'Who made this nucleus? Where did it come from? Who set the Pulsating Universe pulsating in the first place?'

If God made the world, who made God?

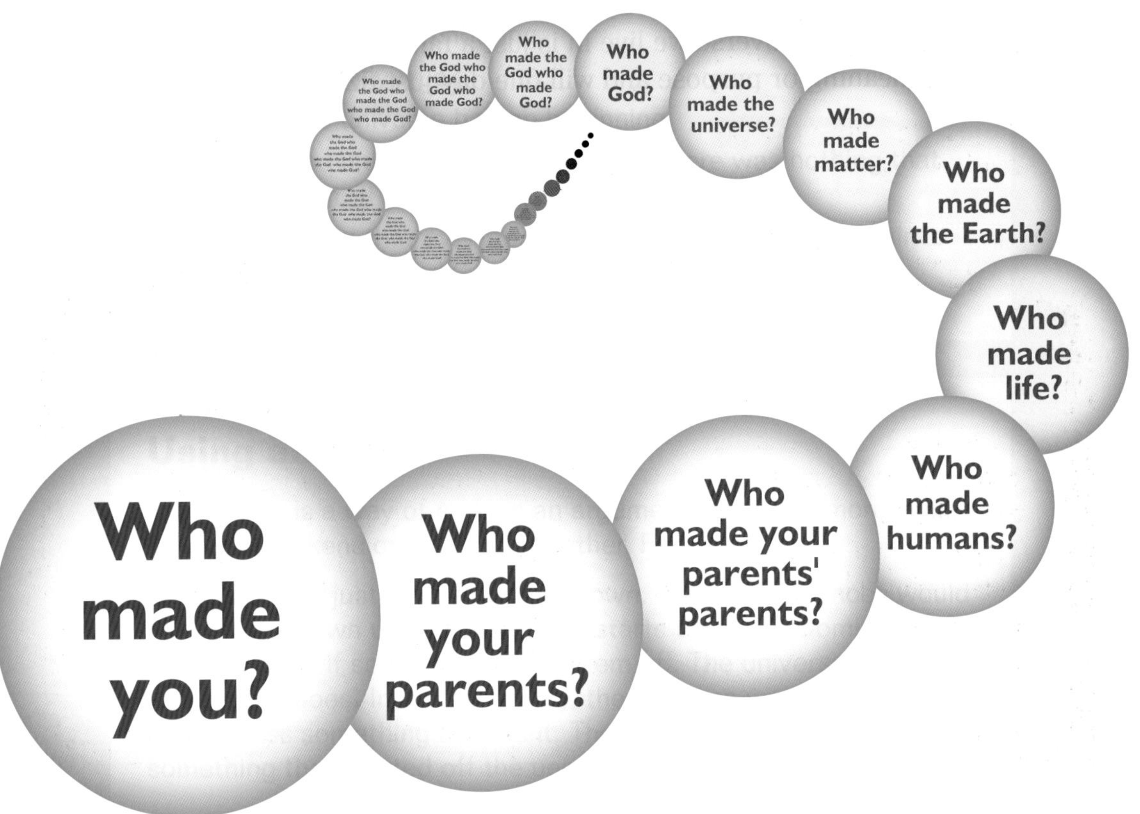

Aquinas' argument is based on the principle 'nothing comes from nothing'. But does Aquinas always keep to this principle? Aquinas claims that things do not just come out of the blue. For there to be something, there must be something that made it happen.

Activity 4 A class debate

Organise a formal class debate. In teams of four, choose a motion to debate: you could use one of the motions suggested below or develop a new motion of your own. You need one team proposing and one team opposing each motion. Suggest a time for any one speaker of between one to two minutes.

This house believes:

a Something made the world and that something was God.

b Religion should never be mentioned in any state funded school in Britain.

c Belief in God is not something you can prove; it is something that you know.

d The world started on its own; there was nothing that caused it to happen.

Activity 5 Research survey

Why do people believe in God?

a Survey the views of your friends and relatives, asking the question, 'In your view, why do people believe in God?'

b Make a record of each person's response to the question. Can their answers be grouped under headings? Draw up a bar chart to show the results of your survey. What conclusions do you think you can draw from your survey?

c You could compare your results to national studies. For example, in the 2001 census, 71 per cent of the UK population described themselves as Christians. However, a Mori poll in 2003 showed that 60 per cent of the British public believed in God, and 29 per cent said they did not. But this was different again from a *New Scientist* poll in 2001 in which 55 per cent of those surveyed thought there was no God. What does this tell you about surveys?

Unit 2
The design argument

The random design game

Below are ten identical long oval shapes and a circle.

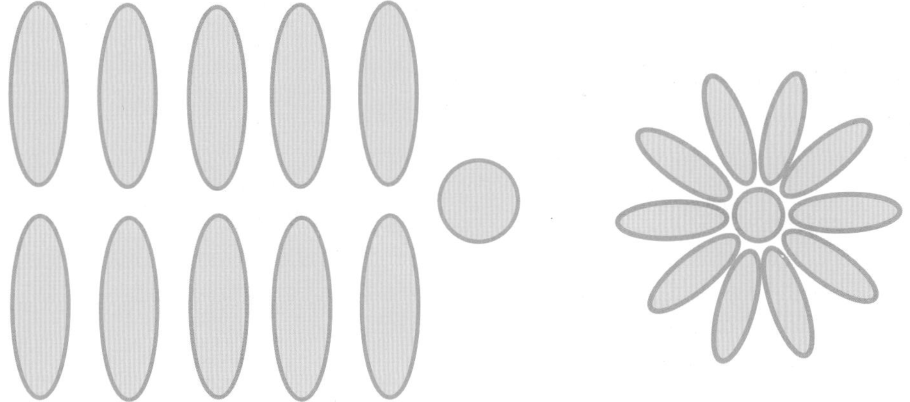

A flower-like pattern.

The daisy: a small European wild flower.

Copy the shapes onto card and cut them out. Now place the shapes into a beaker, shake the beaker and throw the shapes onto a flat surface. You can try this three or four, or even a hundred or a thousand, times until you are bored.

What happens? In every case, you will end up with a random pile of oval shapes and a circle. What never happens (unless you cheat) is for the shapes to neatly fall into a flower-like pattern. They never, for example, fall with the circle in the middle and the oval shapes arranged around the circle.

To create a pattern you have to be careful, neat and deliberate. Flower-like patterns do not come about by random chance. They come about by careful, neat and deliberate design. So how is it we see the same sense of careful, neat and deliberate design in the world around us?

Many natural things have the appearance of being designed. For example, look at the geometric design and order in a daisy, a beehive or in snowflakes. Humans have marvelled at this for thousands of years. Why do things in nature have all the signs of being designed? For many people there is a clear answer to this question. The design we see in nature is no accident. This is the work of a thinking being who made the universe. That being is God.

William Paley (1743–1805)

'The marks of design are too strong to be got over. Design must have had a designer. That designer must have been a person. That person is God.'

William Paley

There are many versions of the design argument for God. One of the best known was written by William Paley. William Paley was a priest in the Church of England. Born in Peterborough in 1743, his book *Natural Theology* (published in 1802) contains his famous 'design argument' based on the idea of the watchmaker. The argument goes something like this:

William Paley's design argument

Suppose you found yourself on a desert island. After exploring the island for a week or so and finding no villages, huts or burger bars, you might conclude that there was no intelligent life on the island, only coconuts and wild animals.

But suppose one day while wandering over your island you found a watch. What would this tell you? Even if you had never seen a watch before in your life, by looking at the incredibly clever miniature wheels, cogs and springs, you would have to say that it was obvious that no plant or animal could have made this mechanism. You would conclude that either there still was, or there had been, intelligent life on the island. You would reason that intelligent life, a watchmaker, had made this watch and it had then been left on the island.

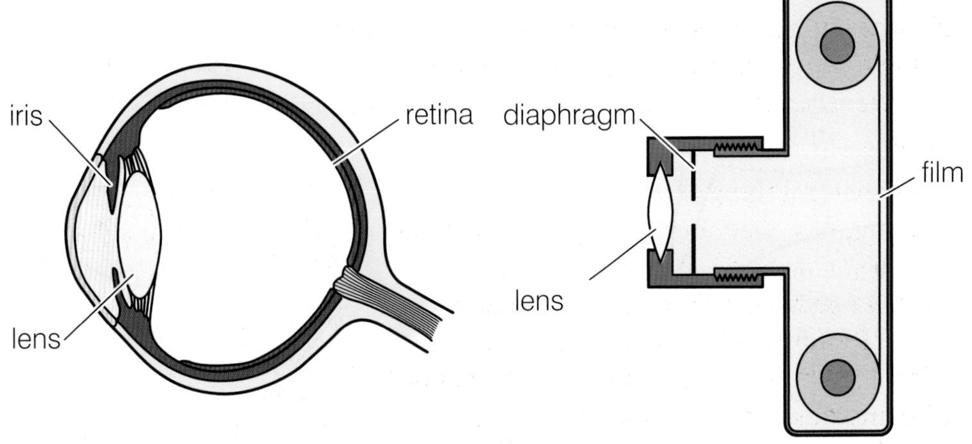

A human eye.

A simple camera.

With this idea in mind, if you look around the world, you will find things that are like a watch on a desert island. An example of this would be the human eye. The human eye in many ways resembles a very well-designed camera.

The human eye has an iris that opens and closes depending on how light or dark it is – just like the diaphragm on a camera.

The eye has a lens that is able to bring things into sharp focus. Little muscles attached to the lens make it fatter or thinner. This makes it possible for the eye to bring things into focus whether they are close up or far away.

The eye has a retina that, like the film in a camera, is light sensitive. These cells can recognise the difference between red, green and blue light, making it possible for us to see in colour.

Like a watch or a camera, the eye is an incredibly clever mechanism. It is obvious the human eye has not come about by some lucky chance. The parts of the human eye have not just been thrown together by accident and so fortunately work. The human eye is a highly efficient and well-designed structure. Design must have had a designer. The designer must have been a person. The design argument says that person is God.

Paley's analogy

Earlier we said 'an analogy is when you suggest a likeness to something else' (see p. 2). William Paley likens a watch to the human eye. A watch cannot design and manufacture itself. Hence there must be a watchmaker. Using the human eye as a similar example, Paley argues the eye cannot design and manufacture itself. Hence there must be an eye designer. That eye designer is God.

Paley gives many examples of great design in the world: the wings on a bird, antennae on an earwig, the fins on a fish. All these examples, Paley claims, proves there must be a great designer. This great designer is God.

David Hume

David Hume was a Scottish philosopher. Twenty years before William Paley wrote his version of the design argument, Hume said that there were big flaws in any argument for God based on design in the universe. Hume wrote his ideas in his book *The Dialogues Concerning Natural Religion*, which was published in 1779. As the book criticised some of the well-known arguments for God, Hume wrote the book in secret. It was published three years after he died.

Hume argued that in the design argument there are a number of hidden assumptions. Here are four:

David Hume (1711–76)

For all we know, 'The world…is very faulty and imperfect…and was only the first essay of some infant deity; who afterwards abandoned it, ashamed of his lame performance.'

Hidden assumptions

1 Even if we agreed that the universe is full of great design, this does not prove that there is only one great designer, God. The hidden assumption is that great design means there must be one great designer. But there could be many gods, all of whom are great designers, all of whom have been busy putting their designs into the universe. The design argument might prove there are many gods. It does not prove there is one God.

2 Even if we agreed that God is the great designer who designed the universe, how do we know that God is still here? The hidden assumption is that God is still with us. Perhaps God designed and made our universe but decided that, as a first attempt, it was a bit of a botch. Who is to say that God has not given up on us and has gone to make a better universe elsewhere?

3 Pointing out examples of what looks like good design like the human eye and a bird's wing is all very well. But the hidden assumption is that good design means that a good God designed the universe. But we cannot know that God is good. Perhaps God is not at all good. Perhaps God is cruel and is merely amusing himself by placing bad design in the world like earthquakes, tsunamis volcanoes, malaria and cholera.

4 Why liken the human eye to a made object like a watch? Why not liken the human eye to something that is not made, like a plant, a dandelion, for example? A dandelion is not made; it grows from seed of its own accord. The hidden assumption is that the human eye is made, but why could a human eye not be like a dandelion and just grow of its own accord?

Hume's ideas have influenced a lot of people, particularly agnostics and atheists. But Hume mainly pointed out that good design in the universe does not logically prove that there has to be a single, good God. Hume did not explain why there was good design in the universe. He just said that God does not have to be the only explanation.

The person who provided a brilliant answer to the question, 'Why is there good design in the universe?' was one of the greatest scientists of all time: Charles Darwin. It was Charles Darwin, much more than David Hume, who really shook the design argument.

Evolution and the design argument

Why do some animals have claws, while other animals have hooves? Why do some animals have long necks, while other animals have big ears? For thousands of years people believed each animal looked the way they did because this was how God had created them in the beginning.

Charles Darwin (1809–82)

'I have called this principle, by which each slight variation, if useful, is preserved, by the term of "natural selection".'

In 1859, Charles Darwin shocked the world with a completely different idea. In his book *The Origin of Species*, Darwin argued that animals and plants had not always looked the way we see them today. He said that species had slowly changed over thousands and thousands of years. What had made these species of animals and plants change was that they had adapted to the world around them in order to survive. This process of adaptation is called 'evolution'.

Darwin argued that what drove this process was competition to survive. Rabbits with big ears and good hearing, according to Darwin, were not a clever example of God's brilliance as a designer. Instead, the theory of evolution suggested that there was a battle for survival going on, which Darwin called 'natural selection'. Here is an example:

Natural selection

Let us assume bigger ears mean better hearing. When a fox goes on the prowl, the rabbits with bigger ears would be the first to hear the fox coming and run for cover. Rabbits with even only slightly smaller ears and hearing that was only slightly less good would be more likely to get eaten. The surviving bigger-eared rabbits would breed more, passing on their slightly bigger ears to their offspring. But foxes who could creep around more quietly would also be doing better than other foxes, so, for rabbits, the pressure to improve their hearing never ends. Over hundreds and thousands of years you end up with what we see today – rabbits with big ears (and very sneaky foxes).

Darwin's ideas seemed to rule out any claim that 'God' was designing animals with special features like good hearing or good eyes. What was happening was a slow process. Rabbits with slightly poorer hearing were being steadily culled, resulting in the survival and growth of rabbits with slightly better hearing. Even more than this, rabbits and, say, deer had both once been the same mousy mammal, and over millions of years random genetic mutations had led to two completely different animal species.

In Darwin's theory there appeared to be an answer to Paley's wonderment over the human eye. Yes, the human eye is a wonderful thing and at first sight you might think, 'How could something like an eye *evolve* – you can either have an eye or you cannot.' But there is an answer to this: a primitive life form might have a patch of cells that, owing to a random mutation, can sense light. That means the creature can tell if it is swimming up to the sunlight or down into the murky ocean depths. After millennia of natural selection, the patch of cells could evolve into something that can see patches of shade well enough to mean it can hide under rocks. Add another few million years and maybe this becomes something that can sense the fuzzy outlines of tasty morsels floating by. You get the idea.

Signs of God

In many of the great religions there is a strong tradition that the natural world provides clear evidence for the existence of God. Often this is called 'natural theology'. In Islam, for example, there is a long established belief that all around us there are clear signs of God. The holy book of Islam, the Qur'an, has over 25 passages that are about 'signs of God'. In the Arabic of the Qur'an these signs are called '**ayats**'. The Qur'an regards these ayats as being such obvious evidence that there is a God that sceptics who do not recognise these signs are described as being wilful and obstinate, intentionally refusing to accept what is plain.

The signs of God that the Qur'an most often refers to are things like:

- the huge variety of animal life around us
- how human life grows inside a mother
- the orderliness of day and night, tides, trade winds and seasons
- life-giving water in the form of rain
- the fertile earth as the source of fruit and crops.

Surah 45:3–5 is a typical example of the Qur'an's account of these signs.

Surely in the heavens and earth
there are signs for believers.
And in your creation and the crawling things
He scatters abroad,
there are signs for people whose faith is sure,
and in the alternation of night and day,
and the provision God sends down from heaven,
and thereby revives the earth after it is dead,
and the ordering of the winds,
there are signs for a people who understand.

Qur'an 45:3–5

And I have felt
A presence that disturbs me with the joy
Of elevated thoughts; a sense sublime
Of something far more deeply interfused,
Whose dwelling is the light of setting suns,
And the round ocean and the living air,
And the blue sky, and in the mind of man...

William Wordsworth (1770–1850)

Perhaps the design argument is more persuasive if the examples used focus on beauty in the world rather than design, which focuses on function. In the magnificent glow of an orange sunset, or in the white magic of moonlight, or in the view across a rolling green valley, many might see the hand of God. At such moments, when time stands still, little else matters, all discussion ceases and proof might not seem necessary.

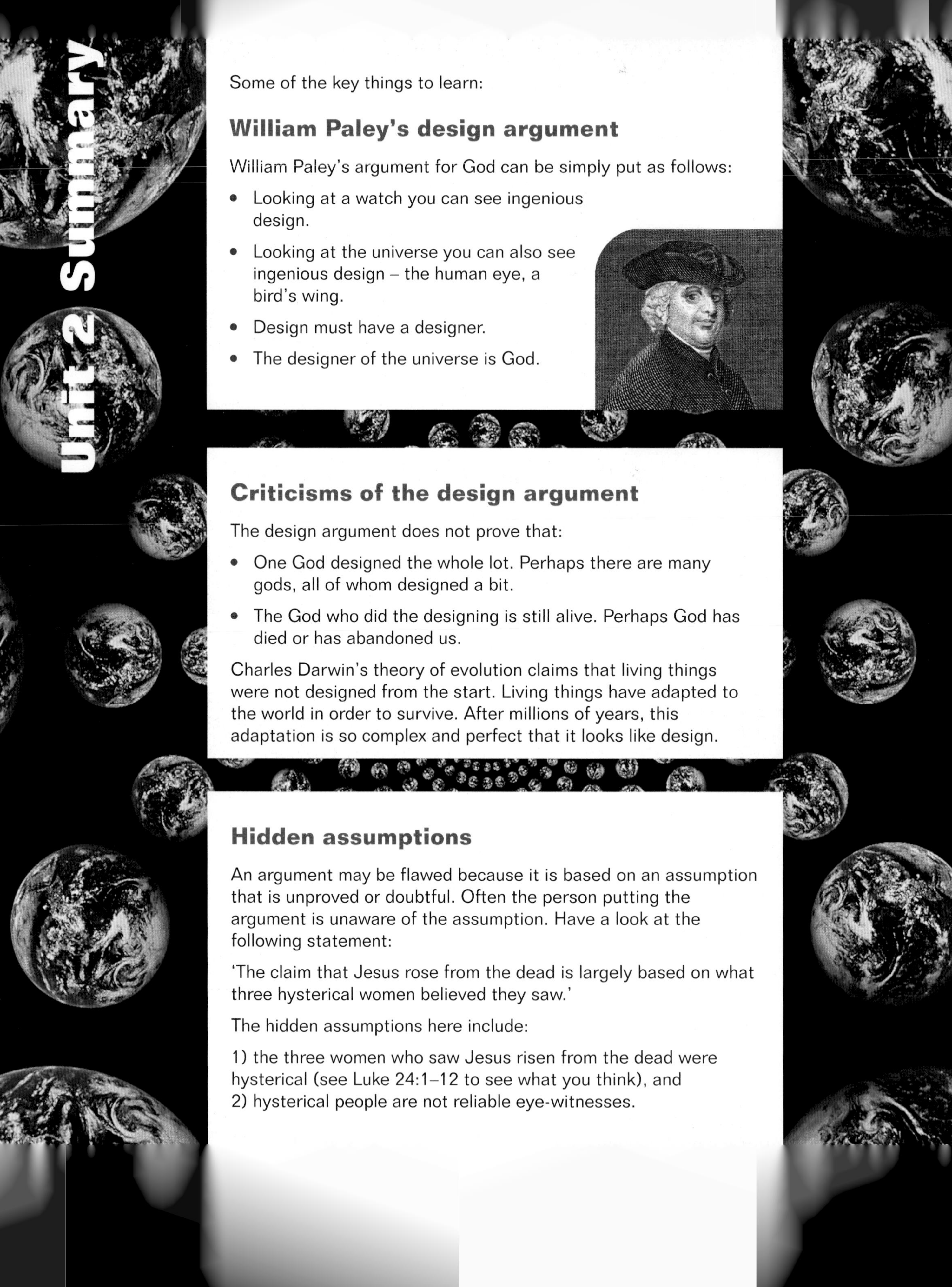

Some of the key things to learn:

William Paley's design argument

William Paley's argument for God can be simply put as follows:

- Looking at a watch you can see ingenious design.
- Looking at the universe you can also see ingenious design – the human eye, a bird's wing.
- Design must have a designer.
- The designer of the universe is God.

Criticisms of the design argument

The design argument does not prove that:

- One God designed the whole lot. Perhaps there are many gods, all of whom designed a bit.
- The God who did the designing is still alive. Perhaps God has died or has abandoned us.

Charles Darwin's theory of evolution claims that living things were not designed from the start. Living things have adapted to the world in order to survive. After millions of years, this adaptation is so complex and perfect that it looks like design.

Hidden assumptions

An argument may be flawed because it is based on an assumption that is unproved or doubtful. Often the person putting the argument is unaware of the assumption. Have a look at the following statement:

'The claim that Jesus rose from the dead is largely based on what three hysterical women believed they saw.'

The hidden assumptions here include:

1) the three women who saw Jesus risen from the dead were hysterical (see Luke 24:1–12 to see what you think), and
2) hysterical people are not reliable eye-witnesses.

Unit 2 Things to do

Activity 1 Pyramid – is there an intelligence behind it all?

a A starfish

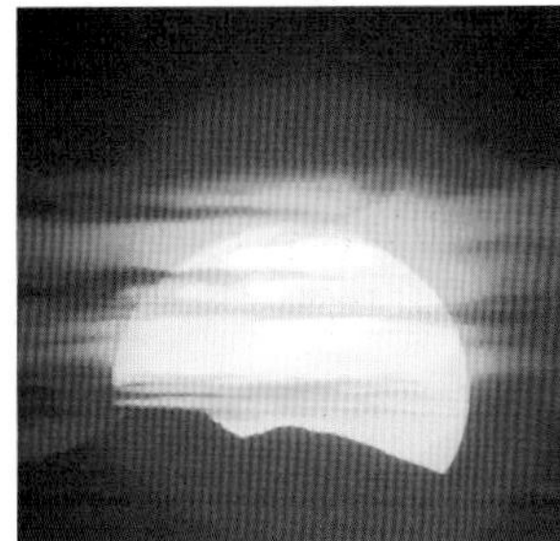
b A sunset

c A water ripple

d A chrysanthemum

e A honeycomb

f A dandelion

In pairs, look over the images above. Arrange the six triangles below into a pyramid with the view you agree with most at the top of the pyramid, your second and third choice underneath, and the three views you least agree with at the base. If you do not agree, talk about why. Give a reason for your first choice. If you do not really agree with any of these views, write a triangle of your own.

These pictures make me think there is an intelligence or something there after all. But I would not call it God. **1**

The world is amazing. It does make me think that there might be a God behind it all. **2**

In nature you can see good evidence of an intelligence at work. **3**

It is not an intelligence that shapes the universe; it is things like gravity and evolution. There is no God. **4**

The world around us is often beautiful. It might suggest that there is a God but it is not likely. **5**

There is an invisible intelligence in the universe and that intelligence is God. **6**

Activity 2 Hidden assumptions

An argument might look correct but it may contain an assumption, or several assumptions. We like to believe that what we think is true and this can prevent us from seeing assumptions in an argument. Sometimes an assumption can be based on a prejudice or on a misunderstanding.

Choose one of the statements below that you think is based on an assumption. What is the hidden assumption?

a We live in a godless society in which no one knows right from wrong.

b Most people believe in God so there must be something in it.

c We know God made man on the sixth day as it says so in the Bible.

d Darwin's theory of evolution is only a theory.

e Humans have been in space for over 40 years but nobody has seen God while up there.

f No God would create a hell in which to torment human beings, that is why there is no God.

g God died of a broken heart because his son was killed on the cross.

Activity 3 Useful words

In the boxes below are four words often used when talking about religious belief.

agnostic **benevolent** **deity** **evolution**

What do these words mean? Which of these words would best finish off the sentences below? Make up a sentence of your own using one of these words.

John Locke (1632–1704)

Robert Millikan (1868–1953)

Charles Darwin (1809–82)

Dennis Potter (1935–94)

Activity 4 A class debate

Organise a formal class debate. In teams of four, choose a motion to debate: you could use one of the motions suggested below or develop a new motion of your own. You need one team proposing and one team opposing each motion. Suggest a time for any one speaker of between one to two minutes.

This house believes:

- **a** The existence of humans can only be explained if there is a God.
- **b** Being agnostic about God is the only view which today makes sense.
- **c** A person with no religion can have no real purpose in life.
- **d** Every British citizen needs to know about the country's main religions.

Unit 3
The moral argument

Questionnaire: What should you do?

Tick the box to say what you *think* you should do. Do not tick what you might do or just what makes for a funny answer.

1 While walking past a bank cash dispenser, you notice £50 left in the machine. Should you:

a grab the money and run? ☐

b take the money into the bank and explain what happened? ☐

c tell your friend to grab the money and split it with them later? ☐

2 Without asking, you have borrowed your elder brother's expensive shirt. While wearing it, you spill a drink and stain it. You try to get the stain out but it is permanent. Should you:

a return the shirt to your brother's room and not say a word? ☐

b own up to your brother and say it was your fault? ☐

c throw the shirt away and not tell your brother? ☐

3 While in a big department store, your friend slips three music CDs into her bag. Should you:

a encourage her to steal two more CDs that you would like to have?

b advise her to put the CDs back before she gets caught?

c tell your friend to cut off the security surveillance tags?

4 While running down a street, your friend collides with a weedy looking new boy. Blaming the new boy for the accident, your friend says he is going to beat him up. Your friend has talked two other boys into helping him and wants to know if you will come as well. Should you:

a join your friend and beat up the new boy good and proper?

b tell your friend it was an accident and he should forget it?

c join your friend enthusiastically and persuade a few more to join in?

5 Your sister bullies your timid cat by throwing it in the garden pond. Should you:

a encourage your sister to bully other family pets as well?

b ask your sister to leave the cat alone?

c join your sister in the bullying of the cat?

6 You raise £40 on a sponsored walk for a local children's hospital. Should you:

a keep £5 and tell the hospital that not all your sponsors paid up?

b hand over all of the £40 to the children's hospital?

c keep the £40 and tell the hospital you earned it so you should keep it?

7 Your father has an argument with a neighbour about his car blocking the drive. Should you:

a take revenge on your neighbour by puncturing his tyres?

b let the matter go and say no more?

c shout and scream at the neighbour?

8 While out shopping, your friend loses all of her money and her mobile. She asks if you can lend her £1.20 so she can get the bus home. You have £15. Should you:

a take the bus home and leave your friend stranded?

b lend your friend £1.20?

c offer to lend your friend £1.20 if she gives you her expensive watch?

9 You see two men clearly stealing objects from your neighbour's house. Should you:

a ask the two men if you can have some of the stuff they are stealing?

b phone the police and tell them that a burglary is taking place?

c wait until the men have gone and then steal from the house yourself?

10 You have been dropped as the freestyle champion by your swimming club. You have been replaced by a new star who is much faster. Should you:

a inflict an injury on the star that will stop them swimming for a bit?

b put on a brave face and keep doing your best?

c hire a killer to 'hit' the star and put them permanently out of action?

Check your point score

1 a 1 point
b 5 points
c 2 points

2 a 1 point
b 5 points
c 2 points

3 a 2 points
b 5 points
c 1 point

4 a 2 points
b 5 points
c 1 point

5 a 1 point
b 5 points
c 2 points

6 a 1 point
b 5 points
c 2 points

7 a 1 point
b 5 points
c 2 points

8 a 2 points
b 5 points
c 1 point

9 a 2 points
b 5 points
c 1 point

10 a 2 points
b 5 points
c 1 point

50 points
Phew…thank goodness! You have a good understanding of the difference between right and wrong. Your moral knowledge is sound and you are safe to walk around and mix with other humans.

49–45 points
What!? Perhaps you did not read the questions properly or did not understand the instructions. Try the questionnaire again.

44–35 points
Trust me on this one, your moral knowledge is on the blink. Lock yourself in a room and wait for the medical team to arrive.

34–25 points
Take it easy. Try and breathe normally. You are not a bad person (yes, I am patronising you) but you are sick. Your understanding of right and wrong is either impaired or it never properly developed. You may be beyond treatment.

24–1
Are you just visiting the planet? You appear to have no moral knowledge and no understanding of right and wrong. You have no respect for others, no regard for the truth and no awareness of the hurt or pain to others your actions might cause. Have you thought about a career in a terrorist organisation or perhaps as a tabloid journalist?

Knowing right from wrong

Knowing what is morally right from wrong is often thought to be very controversial and unclear. That is why there are longstanding arguments about what is right and what is wrong. For example, people disagree over issues like: is it wrong to hunt foxes? Is it sometimes right to go to war? Is abortion always wrong?

Controversial though these questions are, there are many other moral questions that are not at all controversial. Most people would agree that it is wrong to steal what does not belong to you. Most people know that it is wrong to kill someone just because you do not like them.

These examples show that morality, far from being subjective, is often very clearly objective. Some things are right and some things are wrong. It is as if there is a moral law that we all know is true. We all know taking someone else's £50 from a bank cash dispenser is wrong. We may find it hard to resist the temptation, but we know deep inside that taking the money is wrong.

Given that we have this objective moral law, what does this tell us? The fact that there is a clear moral law suggests to some that there is a being that is the source of that moral law. For them, that being is God.

The moral law argument

In his book *The Theory of Good and Evil* (1907), Hastings Rashdall argued that as clear-cut moral knowledge exists, there must also exist a mind whose thoughts are the standard of that moral knowledge. That mind is the source of our moral ideals. That mind is God.

Another way of expressing this moral argument is to suggest that from birth humans are programmed with a knowledge of the moral law: like the way every computer is programmed with certain instructions. Only God would be able to programme us from birth with this moral law. So, for the moral argument, the fact that we are aware of this in-built moral law is evidence of this programming and so is evidence of God.

Hastings Rashdall (1858–1924)

'An absolute moral ideal can exist only in a Mind from which all Reality is derived...in other words, objective morality implies the belief in God.'

Proof and evidence

Suppose Sherlock Holmes looked at the dead body in the library and said, 'The murderer had an accomplice.' Dr Watson might say, 'Astonishing, Holmes! Do you have any proof?' What Dr Watson should have said was, 'Do you have any evidence?' We often use the words 'proof' and 'evidence' as if they have the same meaning. However, they do not strictly speaking mean the same thing.

Proof

The word 'proof' refers to the way in which something is known in a way as to make it **irrefutable**, that is, certain. For example, the ancient Greek mathematician Euclid proved that the sum of the three interior angles of every triangle is equal to two right angles (180°). Euclid's proof is irrefutable. The angles marked b must be equal. Also, the angles marked c must also be equal. The two angles marked a are also obviously equal. Angles $a + b + c$ must therefore equal 180°. It is widely thought that very few things can be 'proved' irrefutably in this Euclidean sense.

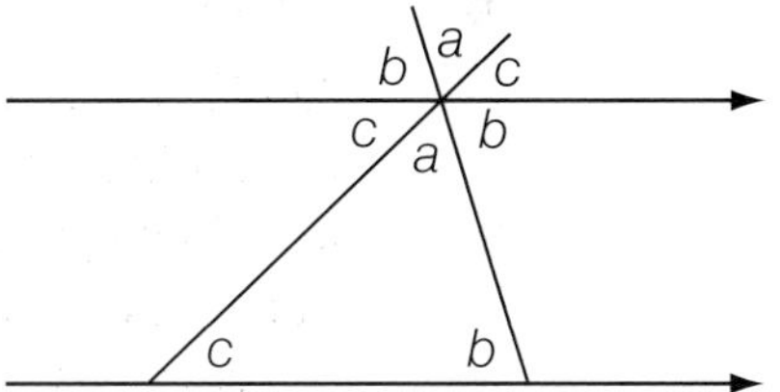

Euclid's proof

(book 1 proposition 32): a + b + c = 180°

Evidence

The word 'evidence' refers to the way in which something is thought to be true because there is good information or signs pointing that way, but this information does not provide an irrefutable proof. For example, Sherlock Holmes might have said to Dr Watson, 'Elementary, my dear Watson. Look here by this open window, you can see two different sets of footprints. Over here you can see two separate brands of cigarettes.' The two sets of footprints and the two brands of cigarettes might be good evidence that two people were involved in the murder, but they do not provide an irrefutable proof.

St Thomas Aquinas and William Paley believed that they had developed an irrefutable proof that there is a God. Hastings Rashdall is being a lot more modest. Rashdall is suggesting that the fact that we have knowledge of an objective moral law is evidence that there is a God. Put this way, it is difficult not to agree that Rashdall has a point.

Hastings Rashdall was not the first person to argue that our knowledge of what is right and wrong suggests that there is a God. In the nineteenth century, a famous British cardinal called John Newman argued that a **guilty conscience** also suggests that there is a God.

The guilty conscience argument

All of us have experienced a guilty conscience at some time. Perhaps when you were much younger you did something that you knew was wrong. Perhaps you broke a neighbour's window and ran away, or stole something from a local shop.

At first, you might have felt smug and quite pleased with yourself, thinking you had got away with it. But after a while, as you thought about what you had done, you began to feel uncomfortable. You kept thinking about what you had done, knowing that it was wrong, and you felt ashamed and worried. You might sense that people know you are guilty. You might frequently hear a small voice in your head telling you, 'It was wrong to run away after breaking Mrs Wilson's window,' or, 'I shouldn't have stolen that DVD.' We call this having a 'guilty conscience' and it is a common experience.

Cardinal John Newman (1801–90)
'If we feel responsibility, are ashamed, are frightened, at transgressing the voice of conscience, this implies that there is One to whom we are responsible.'

Why do we have a guilty conscience if we do something wrong? Cardinal Newman argued that our guilty conscience is God's voice inside our head. As God has programmed us to know right from wrong, whenever we do something wrong our conscience switches on, reminding us of what we *should* have done and making us feel ashamed.

So our conscience is evidence that there is a God. Fear and the sense of guilt after doing something wrong implies that there is a being to whom we are responsible and before whom we are ashamed. That being is God.

The evolution of moral knowledge

The moral law argument is based on the claim that humans have a clear-cut moral knowledge. For example, we know killing another person is wrong. We know stealing is wrong. It is claimed that this sort of clear-cut moral knowledge – killing is wrong, stealing is wrong – is evidence that there is a God.

Edward Wilson (1929–)

Wilson argues that under pressure from natural selection we are genetically wired to be good.

The American zoologist Edward Wilson argues that our moral knowledge does not come from God, it comes from how we have evolved. In his 1975 book *Sociobiology – The New Synthesis*, Wilson argues that, as a species, over millions of years we learnt that we have a much better chance of surviving if we co-operate, help each other out and avoid killing or stealing from each other. So our moral knowledge is no great mystery. As a species, if we had not learnt that it pays to be sociable, we would either be a solitary animal or else extinct.

Imagine the following scene. One and a half million years ago, four of our early ancestors find a forest glade close to a riverbank. Living by the river already is another band of four of our ancient ancestors. What do they do? Do the two bands fight against each other? Do they try and steal from each other?

If they did, what would be the sense in that? By doing so they might weaken both bands so that when the winter comes both bands die

One and a half million years ago.

out. Instead, the two bands learn to work together. They hunt for food, build homes and huddle together for warmth. By doing so they survive.

That willingness to avoid making enemies and working together became part of our instinctive way of behaving. Our feeling that we ought to avoid making enemies, and that we ought to work together, remains a strong instinct inside of us. Our moral values, our feelings of guilt, do not come from God. They are evolved attitudes that have helped us to survive.

The voice of our parents

Evolution is not the only explanation for why we have a conscience. Sigmund Freud, the father of **psychoanalysis**, argued that what we learn from our parents and the society in which we are brought up remains with us throughout our life.

Sigmund Freud (1856–1939)

'Civilisation, therefore, obtains mastery over the individual...by setting up an agency within him to watch over it...'

From an early age we are taught that lying and stealing is wrong. In the main, these early lessons about what is right and wrong remain with us. We may not remember specifically being taught by the society around us or by our parents. What we are taught becomes part of our **unconscious** mind and creates the conscience. This is called **social conditioning**.

If, for some reason, we lie about a friend and get a guilty conscience, this is not because our guilty conscience is the voice of God. It is because our unconscious mind is reminding us of what our parents taught us. This may explain why some people may be cruel and violent and yet suffer no twinges of guilt. The answer is their parents may have beaten them, or neglected them as children, and so they grew up not properly learning that violently attacking another person is wrong.

Social conditioning might also explain why some people's conscience seems to vary. For example, why is it that a child born and brought up on an island of cannibals might happily enjoy eating human meat and not feel any sense of guilt, while a child brought up by non-cannibals and yet forced to eat the same meal might suffer nightmares and a crippling sense of guilt for the rest of their life? If the conscience really was the voice of God, why is it that God's message is not always the same?

Immanuel Kant (1724–1804)

'Therefore the *summum bonum* is possible in the world only on the supposition of a Supreme Being.'

Of course, people like Sigmund Freud and Edward Wilson have not put an end to using morals as an argument for God. Nearly two hundred years ago the great German philosopher Immanuel Kant, in his book *Critique of Practical Reason*, suggested that it is morally necessary to assume the existence of God. Kant's argument is very difficult to follow. Below is one version of the moral argument that uses some of Kant's ideas.

The morally necessary argument

Suppose we lived in a world in which no one believed in God. What would be the motive for doing all those good things that millions of people do in the world today? Why would anyone give up their time working to help the poor and sick? Why would anyone risk his or her own health working in a leprosy hospital? Why would anyone risk being killed standing up against injustice? Most of us avoid killing, stealing and lying. But there are millions of people that set themselves much higher standards. They choose to live lives of goodness way beyond what anyone would expect of them. This is called altruism.

Why would anyone choose to be altruistic? Being altruistic would not guarantee a person happiness. No one would be altruistic if they were told, 'Sacrifice yourself because in the long run we all benefit.' Take, for example, the story of Jackie Pullinger. In 1967, at the age of twenty-three, Jackie Pullinger gave up her comfortable life as a music teacher in London and has spent over 35 years working with heroin addicts in Hong Kong.

Kant's argument is that only a person who believed in God and who believed in a life after death would be prepared to commit themselves in this way. If there was no God, there would be no basis for a true moral life.

Jackie Pullinger (1944–)

'The man asked if I believed in God. "No," I replied, "I know Him, it's different. I know peace, I know where I'm going."'

Working together:

- Work into your argument an analogy to make your argument more vivid.
- Check your argument for any hidden assumptions.
- Support your argument with examples or evidence.
- Have each group report back their argument.

Activity 3 Sort – what sort of judgement?

'Semolina is horrible' is a statement about a person's emotions or personal preferences. It is a judgement based on what a person prefers and so is called 'subjective'. 'Bullying is wrong' is a moral statement. A moral statement is a judgement about what is right or wrong.

It is claimed that moral judgements are not subjective, as they are not merely statements about what a person prefers. Moral judgements, it is claimed, are objective and are not like statements about personal taste.

Tick those statements below which are moral judgements. ☑

Put a 'P' by those statements which are based on taste or personal preference. [P]

1 Modern architecture is awful. ☐
2 I love ice cream. ☐
3 Stealing is wrong. ☐
4 Reality TV is boring. ☐
5 Be as honest as possible. ☐
6 Monet's paintings are beautiful. ☐
7 It is much better to avoid violence. ☐
8 No one has the right to murder. ☐
9 Modern jazz is weird. ☐
10 What Comic Relief does is good. ☐

Activity 4 Nobel Prize

There is a Nobel Prize for peace. Who would you award a Nobel Prize for justice or moral action?

Write down the name of a living, or recently living, well-known person as your nomination. There are some pictures here to start your thinking off, but it could be anyone at all, perhaps someone from your local community, if you like. Place all of the names into a large tin can and shake up the can.

Working in groups of four, randomly pick out four names from the can and agree on one name as your candidate. Prepare a case supporting your candidate. Have each group present their case. Have a vote to decide who should be awarded the prize.

Oscar Schindler

Mother Teresa

Nelson Mandela

Aung San Suu Kyi

Jackie Pullinger

Oscar Romero

Activity 5 A class debate

Organise a formal class debate. In teams of four, choose a motion to debate: you could use one of the motions suggested below or develop a new motion of your own. You need one team proposing and one team opposing each motion. Suggest a time for any one speaker of between one to two minutes.

This house believes:

a If there is no God, then we would not know right from wrong.

b If it were not for religion, there would be few people who would fight against injustice.

c In Britain we are fortunate, as in the main this is a very just and fair society.

d We should not worry about what goes on in the world; everyone should mind their own business.

Unit 4

The religious experience argument

Have you felt a presence or a power?

William James, an American psychologist, was a pioneer in thinking about religious experience. In his book *The Varieties of Religious Experience* (published in 1902), James provides many examples of religious experience. Here is a typical one that happened to a man while hiking in Switzerland:

William James (1842–1910)

'The unreasoned and immediate assurance is the deep thing in us, the reasoned argument is but a surface exhibition.'

'I was in perfect health. We were on our sixth day of tramping. When all at once I experienced a feeling of being raised above myself. I felt the presence of God…I tell of the thing just as I was conscious of it…as if his goodness and his power were penetrating me altogether. The throb of emotion was so violent that I could barely tell the boys to pass on and not wait for me. I sat down on a stone, unable to stand any longer and my eyes overflowed with tears.'

In 1969, the distinguished English scientist Alister Hardy set up The Religious Experience Research Centre in Oxford. Hardy invited the general public to send him descriptions of their own religious experiences. Over the years, the centre has built up a huge archive of such accounts. Here is a typical example:

Alister Hardy (1896–1985)
Religious experience 'is part of the species, a power on which primitive man could draw'.

'The phenomenon invariably occurs out of doors, more often than not when I am alone, though it has occurred when I have been in company. It generally begins with a feeling of…"gladness to be alive". I'm then conscious of an awakening of my senses. Everything becomes suddenly more clearly defined; sights, sounds and smells take on a new meaning. I become aware of the goodness of everything.'

What do these experiences tell us? Firstly, it is clear that religious experiences do not happen only to a few rare individuals in the past. Below are some reminders of famous religious experiences.

Famous religious experiences

The burning bush
1400BCE: Moses hears the voice of God and sees a burning bush.

The Buddha's enlightenment
530BCE: the Buddha achieves enlightenment while meditating under the Bodhi Tree.

Jesus' baptism
27CE: Jesus at his baptism hears a heavenly voice and experiences the presence of the Holy Spirit.

The Day of Pentecost
30CE: The disciples experience the presence of the Holy Spirit.

The road to Damascus
30CE: St Paul is blinded by a light and hears the voice of Christ.

The Night of Power
610CE: Muhammad sees a vision of the Angel Gabriel (Jibril) and is given words of revelation.

The River Bein

1499CE: Guru Nanak experiences God calling him to be God's Guru.

The grotto at Lourdes

11 February 1858: Bernadette Soubirous sees a vision of a lady.

The Day of Inspiration

10 September 1946: while travelling by train, Mother Teresa hears a voice telling her to work with the poor.

Well known though these cases are, the work of William James and Alister Hardy suggests that millions of very ordinary people also have experiences today which are very similar to the experiences of St Paul or Bernadette Soubirous.

In the archives of The Religious Experience Research Centre there are thousands of examples of ordinary people claiming to have experienced God, a presence, or a power in the world. There are others who claim to have seen Jesus, a golden light, a saint, the Virgin Mary, angels, heard a voice or felt they had been called. Others report a sense that everything will be all right, a gladness at being alive or a sudden feeling telling them what they should do with their life.

The religious experience argument

If we see something, is that enough evidence to say that it is real? Think about the following situation:

Did I really see a fox last night?

It is late at night and you cannot sleep. You get out of bed and look out of the window. In the moonlight in your garden you see clearly a fox. The fox is there for about ten seconds and then walks off.

The following day it is not likely that you would be full of doubt wondering, 'Did I really see a fox last night?' You might say to yourself, 'My eyesight is good, the moonlight was fairly bright, the fox was there for quite a while. I was not dreaming, it was not just a shadow: what I saw was a fox.'

If you told your friends, 'I saw a fox in my garden last night,' you would expect your friends to believe you. You might feel a little annoyed if they laughed at you and said, 'Oh yeah…who are you kidding!' You might say, 'Look, I know what I saw, and what I saw was a fox!'

The fact is that the evidence of our senses most of the time is good enough for us to trust what we see or hear is real. If we see flames, or smell smoke, we normally believe what our senses tell us. We would not sit around saying, 'Is this room really on fire? Can I believe the evidence of my senses?'

The religious experience argument takes the same practical approach. If you feel the presence of God, or see an angel, or hear a heavenly voice, such an experience is good enough, says the argument. After the experience you should be able to say, 'I have proof that there is a God. I have had a religious experience and I know God is real.' But could you?

The scientific method

Most of the time we believe the evidence of our senses. But suppose we see something that is very unusual. Suppose instead of a fox in your garden you saw a rhino or an angel! Would you trust your senses? Would your friends believe you?

Francis Bacon was born in London in 1561. Thought by some to be an extraordinary genius, Bacon pioneered what today we call the 'scientific method'. The scientific method relies upon our senses but it does not take our senses for granted. Instead, Bacon said we must find ways of making sure our senses do not deceive us. If we see a fox, a rhino, or an angel in our garden, how can we be sure that what we have seen is true? Bacon did not write about foxes, rhinos or angels in gardens. But we do have a good idea of how he would have thought about the problem. Let us use the fox in the garden example.

Francis Bacon (1561–1626)

'...the human senses and understanding, weak as they are, are not to be deprived of their authority, but to be supplied with helps.'

Sighted 1.42 a.m. 28 June 2005

Sighted 12.07 a.m. 31 June 2005

Sighted 2.18 a.m. 2 July 2005

Sighted 2.43 a.m. 4 July 2005

Many observations are made and are carefully recorded.

The scientific method argument

Many observations

In order to have reliable evidence that there is a fox in your garden, Bacon would have said that a one-off, private sighting just is not good enough. To be more certain that you have not made a mistake, you need to have seen the fox many times. This is why in good laboratories an experiment may be repeated hundreds of times. If you see the same thing again and again, it is less likely that a mistake has been made.

Confirmed by others

To improve the evidence that there is a fox in your garden, it would be better if you were not the only witness. A sighting by one person is always of limited use as evidence. If other people have seen the fox, this again reduces the chances of error. This is why good scientists tell other scientists what they have been doing. The experiment can then be repeated in other laboratories so the results can be confirmed or challenged.

Today, scientists have developed extra ways to improve the scientific method. Good scientists will design experiments using control groups, blind and double blind testing to make sure that their experiments are as fair as possible.

Can religious experience be scientifically tested?

Suppose, instead of a fox, you claimed you saw an angel in your garden. How, using the scientific method, could such a claim be tested? If the angel only appears once or twice and never appears again, how could the claim be confirmed through many observations? If only one person sees the angel, how could others confirm the experience?

The problem with religious experiences is that as they tend to be one-off, private experiences, they cannot be confirmed in the normal scientific way. Although the person who has the experience might be convinced, they are bound to leave others unsure or unwilling to be persuaded.

Generalising from the particular

Francis Bacon helped start a new kind of philosophical approach in Britain. This tradition is called the **empirical tradition** or **empiricism**. The empirical tradition claims that most of our knowledge of the world comes from our senses. However, as Francis Bacon warned, we have to be on our guard to make sure that our senses are not playing tricks on us or that we do not exaggerate what we know.

One error that empiricists often warn we should avoid is making a general claim from a particular case. This is called **generalising from the particular**. For example, if after seeing a fox once or twice, at night in your garden, you told your friends, 'Every night a fox comes into our garden,' this might impress your friends but it is not true. The evidence has been used to make an exaggerated claim. This is an example of generalising from the particular. By taking one or two particular observations, a generalised false conclusion has been made. One or two observations of a fox visiting a garden do not justify the claim that this happens every night.

The vision of Jorgen Wunderboot

A local under-14s football team is having a bad season. The coach tries everything. He trains them hard; they practise their skills and spend hours trying out set moves. They discuss tactics and the coach gives them rousing pep talks. But the team still loses. Determined to turn the season around, the coach comes up with a plan.

At the start of the next game the coach gathers the players together in the changing room. He announces that the team has a special visitor. Into the room walks Jorgen Wunderboot. Jorgen is an international footballing legend and was at the time the manager of one of the great football teams in the country. The kids' mouths drop open.

Jorgen tells the youngsters that he and his scouts have been watching them for some time. He tells them that quite a few of them could be great players. He tells them that he and his scouts will be watching them and he hopes that soon he will be able to sign some of them up for his club.

The youngsters run out onto the field ecstatic. Inspired, they win the game easily 4–0. They play astonishing football for the rest of the season and win both the league and the cup.

What the coach never tells the players is that his old school friend, Fred Nobody, who knows nothing about football, looks exactly like Jorgen Wunderboot. For a fiver, Fred agreed to show up at the changing room and impersonate Jorgen. The youngsters never learnt the truth but some of them did go on to be great players. A few were signed up and played professional football for great clubs.

In the 1948 radio broadcast, Father Copleston put his outcome argument to Bertrand Russell. Bertrand Russell was one of the most important British philosophers of the twentieth century and held well-known agnostic views. Russell argues that however much a religious experience may change or improve a person, it does not alter the fact that the religious experience may not be genuine and is only real in the person's mind.

The all-in-the-mind argument

Suppose, Russell suggests, a young man reads about the life of a great fictional hero. Imagine that the man does not know the book is fiction but takes it to be real. The man may fall in love with the hero in the story and this may have a very good influence on how he lives his life.

However good an influence the fictional hero has on the young man's life does not alter the fact that the hero does not really exist. As Bertrand Russell puts it, 'He's loving a phantom.'

Bertrand Russell (1872–1970)
'You would then be influenced by an object that you'd loved, but it wouldn't be an existing object.'

Bertrand Russell also asks how can you tell whether a religious experience genuinely comes from God, when quite possibly these experiences do not involve the existence of anything outside of ourselves?

A stage hypnotist
It is possible for us to genuinely believe that we can see something that does not exist outside of ourselves.

The unconscious mind argument

Russell did not claim that people who report religious experiences are hallucinating or going insane. It is perfectly possible to be completely sane and yet our unconscious mind might generate an experience that we feel certain comes from God.

A stage hypnotist, for example, might suggest to a volunteer that there is a mouse on the stage. The volunteer may run around the stage to get away from the mouse. The audience may have a good laugh, as they know there is no mouse. The fact that the mouse is a reality in the volunteer's head does not make the mouse real.

Russell himself had had experiences when he felt an overwhelming awareness of what he should do with his life. These experiences altered his character, inspiring him to fight for justice and live a life dedicated to intellectual honesty. Were these religious experiences? Bertrand Russell certainly did not believe they came from God or from anything outside of himself.

Humans are religious animals

In a 1926 essay called *The Vindication of Religion*, A.E. Taylor (1869–1945) claims that only humans are a religious animal. Taylor's argument goes something like this:

The religious animal argument

Just as humans are the only animals that paint and sense beauty, so we are the only religious animal that senses the 'transcendent'.

A human being is, in a sense, a religious animal. Although some of us may know it in only a shallow way, religious experience is the special way in which the whole of life is experienced by humans.

Some may corrupt that experience and end up worshipping money or fame or a football team. But it is doubtful that there is any human who has never worshipped anything. We worship, even though some of us may worship false gods, because worship and religion is in our nature. As the Greeks said, 'Man is the only animal who has gods.'

The only explanation for the special way in which the whole of life is experienced by humans is that God deliberately created us with this nature. Hence there is a God.

Some of the key things to learn:

The religious experience argument

Father Copleston's argument can be put as follows:

- An experience that hugely changes a person spiritually or morally suggests something that brings about such a great change.
- Francis of Assisi changed not because of things going on inside of him. It was something outside of Francis that changed him. That something was God.

Criticisms of the religious experience argument

Bertrand Russell argued that:

- A religious experience may change a person but it does not alter the fact that the religious experience may not be genuine. A fake vision may change a person but the vision would still be a fake.
- Religious experiences are often one-off, private experiences, which cannot be confirmed in the normal scientific way.

Generalising from the particular

Generalising from the particular may lead to a false conclusion. Here is an example:

> 'When my Nan was sick, I prayed really hard and she didn't get better. So I don't think prayer works.'

A general claim is being made about all prayer based on a single, particular case. The general claim about prayer may be true, but the single example given is not enough to make a valid conclusion. If the example is based on a person's own personal experience, it is called **anecdotal**. Anecdotal reasoning may also result in a false conclusion.

Knowing this, God does certain things that go beyond what we normally see going on around us so that we are amazed. These amazing things are what we call miracles. As God is not visible to our eyes, some people are sceptical and do not believe. But miracles are visible. God makes miracles happen so that people may believe. A miracle, then, is a sign of God. Miracles are God's way of rousing our minds so that we see the invisible God in visible things going on around us.

Benedict Spinoza (1632–77)

'Nature cannot be contravened but preserves a fixed and immutable order.'

Do miracles happen?

Augustine's argument explains why God makes miracles happen, but the question still remains: 'Do miracles actually happen?' Augustine answers this question but he does not use a complex philosophical argument.

Augustine believes that miracles are true because he has seen miracles or he has heard witnesses who have seen miracles themselves. When it comes to the Bible, miracles, he says, are also true, adding the comment, 'The Bible does not lie.'

Augustine describes some ten healing miracles he has heard reports on. He had personally witnessed one of these miracles, the case of a respected citizen of Carthage called Innocentius, whose ulcer suddenly disappeared.

For well over a thousand years, most philosophers agreed with Augustine. Most thought that miracles were true. In parts of the world where Christianity was the main religion, the belief that 'the Bible does not lie' was hardly questioned. In 1670, the great Dutch philosopher Benedict Spinoza did argue against miracles in his book *Tractatus Theologico-Politicus*. His book was banned because his religious views were regarded as outrageous.

Sixty years later, in Britain, Thomas Woolston also argued that miracles were not true. He made his arguments in a book called *Six Discourses on the Miracles of Our Saviour* (1727–9). Woolston was convicted of blasphemy and fined. Because he could not pay the bond to promise he would behave himself, he was imprisoned. He died four years later, but it is not clear if he spent those last four years in prison or if he was released and then died a free man.

The healing of a paralysed man (Mark 2:1–12; Matthew 9:1–8; Luke 5:17–26)

Thomas Woolston described this Bible miracle as 'monstrously romantick'.

Being persuasive

Religious issues often arouse strong feelings and deeply felt beliefs. Having a good discussion in these areas involves using special skills like:

- avoiding emotive language (abusive language arouses hostility or resentment)
- focusing on the argument
- not getting personal
- adopting a moderate tone.

In Thomas Woolston's case, he used personal and emotive language. He described Jesus as a 'deceiver, impostor and malefactor'. For Woolston, the resurrection of Jesus was a 'bare-faced…fraud' committed by the disciples.

In amongst this language, any good arguments he made were just not noticed and so he failed to be taken seriously. Fifteen years after Woolston had died, David Hume also argued that miracles were not true. But he used a much more moderate tone. He was not locked up, and although he had many opponents, he was taken seriously.

Hume's book was called *An Enquiry Concerning Human Understanding*. We can call Hume's argument the laws of nature argument.

The blind man at Bethsaida (Mark 8:22–6)

Thomas Woolston said this story makes Jesus look like 'a juggling impostor'.

The laws of nature argument

The feeding of the 5000 (Mark 6:30–44; Matthew 14:13–21; Luke 9:10–17; John 6:1–14)

'A miracle is a violation of the laws of nature…' David Hume

Suppose a friend shows you a loaf of bread, all baked and ready to eat, and tells you that by stretching his hands out and concentrating, he can make the loaf double in size. Clearly this would be a miracle. Loaves simply do not double in size when a person stretches out their hands. If this happened, it would be against the laws of nature.

You might gently humour your friend, suggesting that he ought to lie down. Alternatively, you might challenge your friend to prove his point by going ahead and doubling the size of the loaf. Taking up your challenge, your friend stretches out his hands and concentrates. You stare at the bread, but nothing happens. After several minutes, your friend gives up. Exhausted, he says he is having a bad day and that he will try again.

Your friend may repeat the attempt 50, 60, even a thousand times over the next ten or twenty days, but each time the bread, apart from getting staler, remains completely unchanged. Your friend may be surprised by his lack of success. However, you are not surprised: why not?

The reason why you are not surprised is obvious but it is important. Everyone's common experience is that a loaf of bread does not suddenly double in size when we concentrate hard and stretch out our hands. In no age, and in no country, has anyone been observed making a loaf of bread suddenly double in size. This common experience or law of nature is based on what has happened for thousands of years. This common experience mounts up and provides us with substantial evidence that a loaf of bread simply does not suddenly double in size.

Twelve witnesses against millions

Suppose later you hear reports from witnesses who say that many miles away a man died and was dead for several days and then came back to life again. Should you believe these witnesses? Hume said you should not. Even if you heard twelve witnesses talk of this dead man, you would have to weigh this evidence against the evidence of the laws of nature.

You would ask yourself which is the more likely? Have the twelve witnesses made a mistake and got it wrong? Or is it more likely that what is wrong is our repeated experience, based on what has happened to millions of people for thousands of years, that when you are dead, you stay dead?

The greater likelihood is that the twelve witnesses got it wrong. The laws of nature based on the experience of millions of people for thousands of years is always more likely to be the true answer. Therefore any claimed miracle is always likely to be untrue.

The resurrection (John 20:26–9; Luke 24:39)

'But it is a miracle that a dead man should come to life; because that has never been observed in any age or country.' David Hume

The invisible clockmaker

Inspired by the work of great scientists like Galileo and Isaac Newton, some people came to the view that the universe was like a giant clock. The sun, moon, stars and planets, everything in the universe worked like clockwork. The invisible God had made the clock, had wound it up and had set it running. Once running, God did not interfere or tinker with it with miracles or messages to people. After all, there was no need: the clockwork was perfect – it just kept ticking. These ideas led to the belief in **deism**.

'God, the great architect of nature, has so constructed its machinery, that it never needs to be altered or rectified.' Ethan Allen (1738–89)

Deism: the 'True Religion'

Matthew Tindall (1655–1733) was a teacher at Oxford University and was one of a number of English deists. In his book of 1730, *Christianity as Old as the Creation*, Tindall described what he called the 'True Religion'.

According to Tindall, the True Religion had never been altered or changed since the beginning of time. At its heart, the True Religion involved the belief in the one perfect God. Tindall believed that the main way to worship God was not through religious duties like rituals or ceremonies but by leading a good life. Matthew Tindall rejected miracles, visions or heavenly revelation. In the True Religion there was no claim that Jesus rose from the dead, or that he was the Son of God. There was no faultless holy book, or a revelation from a saviour, a guru or a prophet.

Thomas Paine (1737–1809)
'I believe that religious duties consist in doing justice, loving mercy, and endeavouring to make our fellow creatures happy.'

Deism inspired French philosophers like Voltaire and Rousseau and many of the leaders of the American War of Independence. Men like Thomas Jefferson, Thomas Paine, Ethan Allen and George Washington were all deists.

Deism is often treated as if it died out, but many people today perhaps have deistic ideas although they have never heard the word 'deism'.

Miracles are reasonable

Hume's argument against miracles led to a number of attempts to prove that Hume was wrong. Perhaps the most famous of these is to be found in William Paley's book *A View of the Evidences of Christianity*, which was published in 1794. We have met William Paley earlier when we looked at his design argument (see p. 12).

'In a word, once believe that there is a God, and miracles are not incredible.' William Paley

Paley did not claim that he could prove that miracles were true. However, he did claim that there were very good reasons for believing in miracles. Let us look at two of his arguments: his God hypothesis argument and his honest witnesses argument.

The God hypothesis argument

For the sake of argument, let us suppose there is a God. This is called a **hypothesis**. If there is a God, is it not likely that, at certain important occasions, God may interrupt the laws of nature and make a miracle happen? These interruptions will always be rare and will only be seen by a few. These do not alter or permanently change the laws of nature. They are just rare interruptions.

So, for example, suppose God wants to bring a uniquely special man back to life because this particular man is the Saviour and the Son of God. Given the situation, it is reasonable that God will interrupt the laws of nature and make it happen. In other words, if we accept that there is a God, it is reasonable to accept that there will be miracles.

Mind and body – it is psychosomatic!

Without such clinical reports, the Bible's healing miracles could be explained as examples of **psychosomatic** cures. The word 'psychosomatic' became widely used following the work of the American doctor, Helen Flanders Dunbar.

In her book *Mind and Body: Psychosomatic Medicine* (published in 1947), Helen Dunbar showed that about a third of patients who said they were in pain or were seriously ill when examined by their doctor had nothing physically wrong with them. The illness was 'in their head'.

That is not to say that such people are insane. What it does show is that somehow the mind can unconsciously create symptoms that look like a physical illness. Soldiers who are 'shell-shocked', for example, can experience years of blindness even though, physically, there is nothing wrong with their eyes. Their mind tells them they cannot see and so they cannot see.

Helen Flanders Dunbar (1902–59)

'The sufferers lose their symptoms when their personality difficulties are remedied.'

If the mind can have such a powerful impact on the body, why should it not also be the case that the mind may be telling some people, 'Your legs are paralysed,' or 'You have rheumatoid arthritis'? And if the mind can generate such symptoms, why can it not be the case that the mind can rapidly make such symptoms disappear?

It has been suggested that the apparent success of faith healers in 'curing' sick people can be explained if the people they help are actually suffering from something psychosomatic.

The case of Jean-Pierre Bely

Lourdes often comes up in any discussion on whether miracles happen or not. Lourdes is in the south of France. It became a place of Christian pilgrimage in 1858 soon after it was reported that a fourteen-year-old girl, Bernadette Soubirous, had seen visions of the Virgin Mary (see p. 44). Since then, over 6500 people claim to have been miraculously cured at Lourdes. Anxious to avoid any accusations of fraud, the Roman Catholic Church has declared only 66 of these cases to be officially miracles. The 66th case was that of Jean-Pierre Bely.

Harry Edwards (1893–1976)

During the 1950s, 60s and early 70s, Harry Edwards held large public demonstrations of apparent faith healing. He never charged for his services.

Jean-Pierre Bely first noticed pain and loss of feeling in his fingers and toes in 1972 when he was 36 years old. Over the years, the symptoms grew worse and he was diagnosed with multiple sclerosis in 1984. He was 48 years old. The disease is a neurological condition that progressively paralyses the body. There is no known cure and it often leads to death. By 1985, Jean-Pierre was confined to a wheelchair and the following year he was unable to get out of bed unaided.

The grotto at Lourdes

The 66th official cure that took place at Lourdes was of Jean-Pierre Bely, who stopped suffering from multiple sclerosis in 1987.

In 1987, his friends persuaded him to go to Lourdes. About 5 million pilgrims visit Lourdes every year. In October 1987, Jean-Pierre arrived in Lourdes. Soon after checking in at the hospital, he was taken down to the shrine and received Holy Communion. Later that day while back in the hospital something strange seemed to happen. He felt at first very cold and then very hot. He heard a voice come into his mind saying, 'Get up and walk.' The following night he swung his legs out of the hospital bed and took a few steps. He had not walked for two years before that. The night nurse was astonished. He rapidly made progress and within a few days he could walk, run and ride a bike.

The Medical Committee based at Lourdes and the Roman Catholic Church never rush to a quick judgement in such cases. After twelve years of detailed medical and psychological examination to ensure that there was no other explanation or relapse of his condition, in 1999 the Church declared the cure to be a miracle.

A Catholic bishop called Claude Dagens said, 'This recovery can be considered a personal gift from God for this man, like an act of grace and a sign of Christ the Saviour.' For many people, Jean-Pierre Bely and cases like his are a mysterious sign that there is a God.

Unit 5 Summary

Some of the key things to learn:

The miracle argument for God

St Augustine's argument for God can be simply put as follows:

Miracles, like the sun coming up, happen every day. But we take such things for granted. Because of this, God does certain amazing things that go beyond what we normally see. These amazing things are miracles. Miracles are God's way of rousing our minds and giving us a sign that there is a God.

Criticisms of the miracle argument

David Hume argued that:

Miracles go against the laws of nature. The laws of nature are based on the common experience of millions of people. What a few witnesses to a miracle claim to have seen, when weighed against the common experience of millions of people, must mean it is more likely that the few witnesses got it wrong.

Being persuasive

An argument can be ineffective if it relies on emotive language or personal abuse. A moderate tone is often much more persuasive.

Emotive language:

- 'The resurrection is a lie and anybody who cannot see that makes me sick.'
- 'There is a God. People who do not believe are disgusting and do not have any values.'

Being personal:

- 'If you believe in miracles, then you must be stupid.'

Unit 5 Things to do

Activity 1 Pyramid – what is a miracle?

Arrange the six triangles below into a pyramid with the view you agree with most at the top of the pyramid, your second and third choice underneath, and the three views you least agree with at the base. If you do not agree, talk about why. Give a reason for your first choice. If you do not really agree with any of these views, write a triangle of your own.

Are some of these clearly not miracles? If so, explain why.

1. A miracle has to break the laws of nature, like when Jesus walked on water.
2. The discovery of antibiotics, which has saved many lives – that is a miracle.
3. If you fell out of a window and survived by landing on a bush – that is a miracle.
4. A sunrise or the birth of a baby are amazing and are true miracles.
5. When you press a switch and make a light bulb come on – that is a miracle.
6. When a brutal criminal reforms and becomes a good citizen – that is a miracle.

Activity 2 Continuum

St Augustine

Statue of Christ that bled, Pennsylvania, USA

In 1975, a 28-inch plaster statue of Christ oozed blood from its hands.

Padre Pio

Padre Pio appeared to bear the same wounds as Christ. His hands bled regularly for over 30 years.

'Many miracles have occurred.'

Do you agree or disagree with St Augustine's claim?

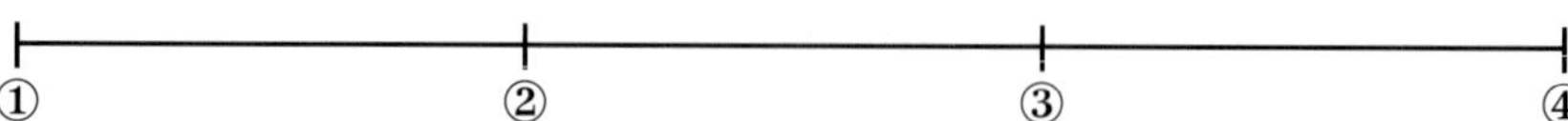

①	②	③	④
Disagree a lot. No miracles have occurred. There is no God so there are no miracles.	Disagree partly. Extraordinary things happen but they are unlikely to be caused by God.	Agree but not fully. Some miracles may have occurred. Perhaps sometimes God sends a sign.	Agree. Many miracles have occurred. Miracles are a sign that there is a God.

Which of these responses do you agree with most? Do you think the responses should be changed? On a score of ① to ④, rate your response and write your number on a piece of paper. Place all the papers into a box and shake them up. Have everyone take out one of the papers. Ask everyone with number ① to form a line so as to make a human bar chart. Do the same for ②, ③ and ④.

In groups, brainstorm reasons or ideas that support one of these views.

Activity 3 Emotive language

In order to persuade it is often best to avoid language that is highly emotive. For example, the statement 'religion is boring' uses the fairly abusive word 'boring'. Whereas the statement 'religion has no interest for many people' is a good deal less abusive or offensive.

Choose two of the statements below. Reword the statements so as to make them less emotive or abusive.

a According to some people who do not believe in the Bible, our ancestors were monkeys.

b The people who said they saw Jesus after he had died must be mental.

c Many religious people say that experimenting on animals is disgusting.

d You have got to be a bit cranky in the head to take miracles seriously.

e Many young people today are yobs who hang around with nothing to do.

f In some religions they worship loads of gods and have funny statues.

g People who meditate sit around and contemplate their navel.

h Many of those who preach sermons do not live in the real world; most of them are old or senile.

Activity 4 Useful words

In the boxes below are three words. What do these words mean? Which of these words would best fit into the sentences below? Make up a sentence of your own using one of these words.

deist **revelation** **psychosomatic**

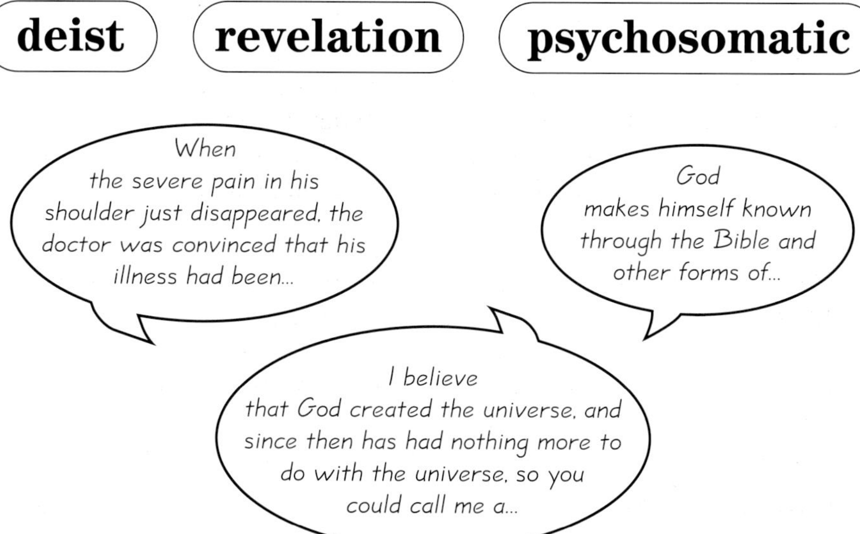

Activity 5 A class debate

Organise a formal class debate. In teams of four, choose a motion to debate: you could use one of the motions suggested below or develop a new motion of your own. You need one team proposing and one team opposing each motion. Suggest a time for any one speaker of between one to two minutes.

This house believes:

a Something immensely impressive happened soon after Jesus' death, which restored the disciples' faith in him.

b One day humans will be able to explain what happens at Lourdes and the answer will not be God.

c You can be a religious person but still not believe in miracles.

d People who write books and plays have a right to be offensive about religion.

Unit 6
The problem of evil

In the early hours of Thursday 18 November 1993, a school minibus was being driven along the M40 motorway. Driving the bus was a very dedicated music teacher. On board were fourteen school children aged between twelve and fourteen. All of the children attended Hagley Roman Catholic High School. A number of them were highly talented musicians. They were returning from London after earlier enjoying a music concert at the Albert Hall. Just after midnight, 30 miles from home, the minibus veered off the motorway and smashed into the back of a parked maintenance lorry. The minibus burst into flames. The teacher and twelve of the children lost their lives.

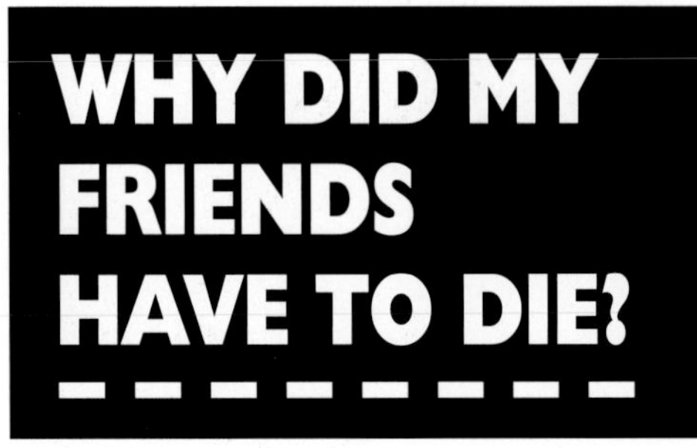

'Either God cannot abolish evil or he will not; if he cannot, then he is not all-powerful, and if he will not, then he is not all-good.' St Augustine

The following day the whole school was in shock. There were tears, and grief was written on the faces of many of the youngsters. As she prepared to attend the morning assembly, one girl asked, 'How could God do this?'

How could God do this?

This is a question countless millions of people have asked following a tragedy. After all, if God is good and is all-powerful, surely God has the power to prevent a senseless minibus accident? Why would an all-loving God want to bring into the world twelve talented young people, only to snuff out their lives before that talent can be realised? What would it have cost God to have done something so that the accident never happened?

Could God not have made a slight bump in the road so that the minibus had jolted and alerted the occupants in the minibus to the danger? If God as an 'act of grace' can cure a man of multiple sclerosis, could God not have planted an idea in the mind of the maintenance lorry driver so that he parked the lorry on a slip road that night and not on the hard shoulder? Could God not have caused the minibus to have a flat tyre shortly before the scene of the accident so that the minibus, after having the tyre replaced, had slowly and safely driven past the maintenance lorry?

Nothing ridiculous – it would not have needed a giant hand to miraculously come out of the sky and nudge the minibus away from danger. There are a hundred inconspicuous ways in which an all-powerful God could have done something.

Are there not inconspicuous ways in which God can prevent terrible tragedies?

Yet God appears to have sat back and done nothing. What are we to make of this? That God is not a caring God after all? That God is cold and indifferent and is prepared to watch while thirteen innocent lives go up in flames? Or perhaps God is not the all-powerful God described in religions like Islam, Christianity and Judaism. God has only limited powers and has to look on helplessly, unable to prevent a minibus ploughing into a stationary vehicle. Sixteen hundred years ago, St Augustine put the issue into a single sentence:

'Either God cannot abolish evil or he will not; if he cannot, then he is not all-powerful, and if he will not, then he is not all-good.'

The argument against God

The fact that evil things happen and how that can be squared with the belief that there is an all-powerful and loving God is known as the **problem of evil**. The problem of evil raises serious questions like, 'What is God up to?' 'Why does God not get rid of evil in the world?' and 'Is there a God at all?'

John Stuart Mill was one of the leading English philosophers of the nineteenth century. He did not believe in God. In his book *Nature and Utility of Religion*, which was published in 1874, he argued that any reasonable look at the world suggests that there is no God in control.

John Stuart Mill (1806–73)

'Everything, in short, which the men commit either against life or property is perpetrated on a larger scale by natural agents.'

The cruel world argument

Nature is reckless and indifferent to life. Nature is often cruel. It not only takes life, it also takes the means to life. A single hurricane, or a flood, or a swarm of locusts can destroy a whole season's crops, leaving millions of people to struggle in poverty and slow starvation. Humans are responsible for many evil things in the world like murder, war, torture and exploitation. However, all that is nothing compared to the daily murder and torture people suffer due to diseases like cholera, malaria and typhoid.

There is no sense in which this misery is evenly distributed to people who live on this planet so that we can see any justice. It is always the poor who suffer disease, natural disasters and starvation. Only the most distorted view could lead one to suppose that the world was made, or is being governed, by a good and all-powerful God.

'Not even on the most distorted and contracted theory of good...can the government of nature be made to resemble the work of a being at once good and omnipotent...' John Stuart Mill

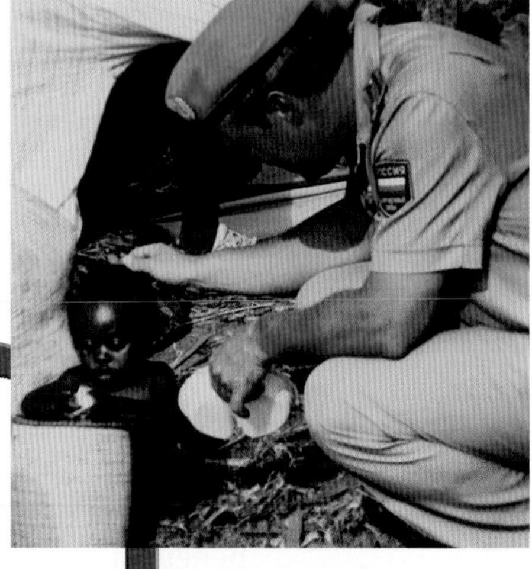

The devil's fault argument

The belief that evil is the devil's fault is an ancient idea at least two and a half thousand years old. One of its most famous teachers was Zoroaster. Zoroaster was a religious teacher who lived in Persia some five hundred years before Jesus. Zoroaster taught that there are two main forces in the universe: good and evil. The evil force or spirit was called Ahriman. The good force was a God called Ahura Mazdah.

The forces of good and evil permanently battle against each other. In this battle, evil may for a while get the upper hand. When that happens, Ahriman is free to inflict evil like an awful road accident or cause people to starve. But the great God Ahura Mazdah is always there, battling against evil. Zoroaster taught that good and evil are pretty closely matched.

Zoroaster (Zarathustra) (628–551 BCE)

'The two spirits which appeared in the world of thought in the beginning were good and evil thoughts, words and deeds.'

Zoroaster's idea of two forces, good and evil, which are closely matched, is called **dualism**. Dualistic ideas often form the basis of many popular books and films, for example the *Star Wars*, *Lord of the Rings*, *Harry Potter* and *The Matrix* films.

Monotheism and the devil

Many religions are **monotheistic**. That is, they teach that there is only one God.

Monotheistic religions like Islam, Judaism or Christianity have a problem if they try and claim that evil is the devil's fault. The German philosopher Friedrich Schleiermacher made this clear with his 'Who made the devil?' argument. He expressed his argument in his book *The Christian Faith*, which was published in 1821.

Friedrich Schleiermacher (1768–1834)

'The idea of the devil is so unstable that we cannot expect anyone to be convinced of its truth.'

The 'Who made the devil?' argument

Monotheists believe in one God, and that God is the creator of everything. In the Bible it says, 'In the beginning there was nothing.' If God made the world from nothing, then who made the devil? It must have been God. The devil did not exist before creation, as there was nothing. As God created everything, then it must be that God created the devil. If God did create the devil, then God has to take a lot of the blame for what the devil does.

To get around the problem it might be claimed that God did not make the devil but that the devil, like God, has always existed. After God had made the world, the devil came out of the shadows and brought evil into the world. Ever since, God has been battling against the devil.

The trouble with this idea is that it does not look like one supreme, all-powerful God after all. It looks as if there is a good God up against an evil God, and their powers are pretty closely matched. Instead of one supreme God, it looks as if there are two rival Gods.

That said, many atheists, agnostics and Christians have concluded that the story of Adam and Eve and the Fall is not after all history. The Adam and Eve story for them is an example of a **religious myth**. A religious myth does not describe real events or real people. Instead, religious myth helps to express religious ideas or beliefs through imaginative images. A religious myth may express a 'truth' about life, God or human nature.

John Hick (1922–)

'But the time has long been with us when Christians...must frankly say that the Genesis story is not history but myth.'

One leading British religious philosopher, John Hick, said that what religious myth did was 'illumine by means of unforgettable imagery'. (He said this in *Evil and the God of Love*, published in 1966.)

Adam and Eve, then, might not be 'true' historically but that did not take away from the fact that it might be illuminating a profound religious 'truth'. That 'truth' or message might be something like the following:

We humans live in a world that is not perfect and is somehow always wrong for us. This always leaves us unfulfilled. With God's help we will find a way of living as God intended. When we do, we will be with God and our nature will be fulfilled.

The 'truth' of Adam and Eve is not about the past; it is about who we are and where we are heading. Even though the story of Adam and Eve as historical 'truth' might be rejected, its religious 'truth' may always be valid.

Myth is often used in religious philosophy to illuminate an idea. The following 'toy story myth' might help us to see the free will argument in a clearer light.

The toy story myth

Andy has many cool toys. One of his best toys was a radio-controlled toy car. Using the handset, Andy could make the car go forward, backward, right or left. He could make it go fast or slow or spin in a circle. All the time he had control.

One day, Andy drove the car into the neighbour's cat. His mum did not blame the car; she blamed Andy. She said, 'Andy, you are in control.' On another day, Andy used the car to deliver to his mum some flowers he had bought for her on Mother's Day. Andy's mum did not thank the car; she thanked Andy. The car was never blamed or thanked for anything. The car was never right or wrong.

Andy's radio-controlled car.

One afternoon, a nerdy friend tinkered with Andy's toy car. When the friend had finished, Andy found the car drove itself. However much Andy moved the buttons on the handset, the car did its own thing. However, the car did not just drive around and crash into things. When it came to a chair leg, it went around it. When it was on a steep slope, it slowed down. When it came to a wall, it turned around.

The car did other strange things. When the neighbour's mad dog got out and barked and snarled at Andy, without Andy doing a thing, the car powered up and drove over to the dog. The car revved its engine and sounded its horn at the dog. The dog was startled and ran away. Then, while Andy was lying in the hot sunshine, the car drove over and raised its spoiler, protecting Andy from the glare of the sun.

When Andy talked to his nerdy friend about the car, he asked if the car was programmed to do those things. The friend said, 'No, Andy, the car is programmed to have free will. It can choose to do what it likes.'

Although Andy had no control of the car, he found that he liked his free will car much more. The car was now courageous, loyal, thoughtful, imaginative, generous and patient. Andy loved his free will car in a way that was different from all his other toys. For Andy, the free will car was so special that it was not like any of the other toys. For Andy, it was not like a toy. It was much more than that. If anything, it was more like Andy.

Natural evil and moral evil

Below are four pictures. They all show evil. Which is the odd one out?

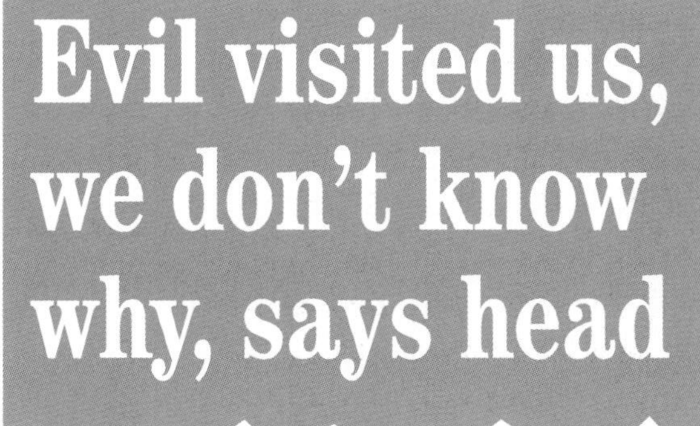

a Murder

b Earthquake

c Flood

d Hurricane

You may have your own ingenious answer to the question, 'Which is the odd one out?' Pictures b, c and d are natural disasters. Picture a is about the shooting dead of sixteen children and their classroom teacher in a school in Dunblane, in Scotland, in 1996. The German philosopher Gottfried Leibniz called evil of this sort **moral evil**. Moral evil is when humans are the main cause of the evil. Moral evil includes things like murder, war, torture, persecution, genocide, exploitation, poverty and injustice.

Leibniz, however, said that there was plenty of evil in the world for which it is difficult to blame humans. He had in mind natural disasters like earthquakes, floods, droughts, volcanoes and hurricanes.

Gottfried Leibniz (1646–1716)

'Evil consists in...physical evil in suffering, and in moral evil in sin.'

Apart from getting in the way and ending up as victims, how could humans be seriously blamed for natural disasters? After all, earthquakes and floods were happening on this planet long before humans appeared. Whether humans do or do not have free will would not stop an earthquake bringing death and misery to thousands.

Another source of suffering is due to sickness and disease. In the world there are millions of viruses and bacteria that directly cause suffering and death. The parasite that causes malaria is thought to kill about 2 million people every year. Humans cannot be blamed for all the disease in the world. Lack of hospitals, doctors, health officials, poor sanitation, lack of clean water, might be part of the problem. However, when a baby is born with a genetic condition like brittle bone syndrome, blaming humans and saying it is all down to free will seems unfair. Leibniz's term for evil that, in the main, could not be blamed on humans was 'physical evil', but usually today it is called **natural evil**.

In 1755, a terrible disaster took place. An earthquake destroyed two-thirds of the city of Lisbon. The disaster did not just destroy a city and take the lives of thousands. It destroyed the optimistic faith of millions of people.

Unit 6 Summary

Some of the key things to learn:

The problem of evil

If God is all-powerful, then God must have the power to stop evil. If God is all-loving, then God must want to stop evil. So why is there evil in the world?

- Control arguments – are based on the idea that God does not have complete control over what happens in the world.
- The devil's fault – evil comes from the devil. God fights against the devil but cannot stop all of the devil's evil.

The free will argument

St Augustine's answer to the problem of evil is based on the idea of free will.

God gave humans free will. God wants humans to be good but God cannot force us to be good. If God forced us to be good, it would only be a fake goodness. We would not really be good, we would be like puppets. The inevitable price we pay is that some people misuse their free will and do evil things.

Myth and story

- Creationists believe that the Bible's account of creation describes historical events.
- John Hick, and many others, believe the Bible's account of creation is not history but myth.
- Myth can be a vivid way of getting across a difficult idea or a profound 'truth'. It can 'illumine by means of unforgettable imagery'.
- Using a story or myth can make an idea clearer. It can make an argument more interesting and more persuasive.

Unit 6 Things to do

Activity 1 Odd one out

With a partner, look at the three images below. Which is the odd one out? There are no right or wrong answers to this question but do think of a reason to support your answer.

Activity 2 The language of respect

From the statements below:

- choose six that may be used to disagree and yet do show respect
- choose six that do not show respect and may cause offence.

a I think the point you are making is important, but I would add…

b You do not seem to understand. The real point is…

c That just shows your ignorance. The truth of the matter is…

d I agree with some of the things you have said, but I think…

e A lot of what you were saying is true, but is it not also true to say…

f As you are a male it is difficult for you to appreciate this, but the truth is…

g I understand why you have that view, but I think…

h That is a dumb view. I think that…

i I think that is wrong. I would say…

j Why don't you shut up and let someone else speak…

k I would agree with your main argument, but I think it also needs to be said…

l That is not a view which I share, as I believe…

m Being female, I understand why you have a different view, but I would say…

n I do not agree with that view. My own view is…

o I find it hard to agree with the points you are making. I would say that…

p Obviously you do not really know what you are talking about. Most people think…

Activity 3 Community of enquiry

Think about the image on the right for about two minutes.

a With a partner, decide on a question that this image raises for you. List all the questions on the notice board for everyone to see. Have a vote to decide which question everyone will discuss. Have about one minute thinking time to decide what sort of things you want to say during the discussion.

b As a class, sit in a large circle. Each person in the circle needs three 'speak cards'. Every time you speak, you use up one of your speak cards. A volunteer needs to comment after the discussion on whether people listened effectively to the views of others and whether this affected what they said. A second volunteer needs to comment on whether respectful language was used.

One person will need to chair the discussion. If that is you, explain that as a community of enquiry this is your discussion. You are listening and supporting the discussion but not speaking yourself.

Activity 4 Useful words

What do the words in the boxes mean? Use the words to write a caption for each of the pictures below.

myth **dualism** **monotheism**

The wrath of God argument

The wrath of God argument claims that evil is an instrument that God uses to justly punish human wickedness. Lisbon, it was claimed, was a very wicked city. Its destruction was God's moral judgement on a sinful city.

The same idea appears in the Bible story of Sodom and Gomorrah. God, we are told, brings down 'brimstone and fire' and destroys the two cities of Sodom and Gomorrah as the people of these two cities are judged to be wicked.

'Then the Lord rained down burning sulphur on Sodom and Gomorrah.' Genesis 19:24

Another instrument argument that is found in both the Bible and the Qur'an is the 'God is testing us' argument.

The 'God is testing us' argument

This argument claims that God uses evil to test our faith. Faith in God is easy if life is very comfortable and without hardship. But how strong is our faith really? To make sure that faith is more than a convenient sham, or a shallow custom, God puts faith to the test.

If we suffer a disaster and lose faith in God, then our faith is exposed as being weak and inadequate. If, however, our faith remains strong even when things go badly wrong, then we have proved that our faith is strong and true.

The argument is found in the Bible: Abraham, for example, is put to the test, having to face the agony of sacrificing his only son.

The same argument is found throughout the Qur'an. For example, the Qur'an says:

> 'and we test you with evil and with good as a trial…' (Surah 21:36)

'Some time later God tested Abraham…"Take your son, your only son, Isaac."' Genesis 22:1

Abu Hamid al-Ghazali (1058–1111) is one of the most celebrated of all Muslim philosophers. In one of his best-known books, *The Revival of the Religious Sciences*, al-Ghazali does not blame the devil or human free will for evil. He accepts that as God is omnipotent then 'pain and anguish is also created by the Lord'. He argues that 'faith is tested through trial'. When faced with this trial he says that 'one should stand firm'.

Enduring troubles with fortitude, or **sabr**, is an important part of al-Ghazali's understanding of Islam. For al-Ghazali, sabr is one of the great qualities all Muslims should strive to develop.

Instrument arguments – the problem

The claim that God is punishing us or testing us raises a tricky problem. If God really is testing or sometimes punishing us, then can God really be called good?

Islam, Christianity and Judaism all claim that God is not selfish, mean-minded or brutal. Instead, God is meant to be good, just, forgiving and benevolent. If God is benevolent, then ultimately everything that happens in the world is for the best.

Voltaire (1694–1778)

'Doubt is not a pleasant condition but certainty is an absurd one.'

Inexcusable evil

Voltaire, the French philosopher, wrote a poem soon after the Lisbon earthquake. In this poem he mocked the idea that everything that happens in the world is for the best. For Voltaire, the idea that those who died in Lisbon were sinners who were justly the victims of God's anger was absurd. He ridiculed the claim that disasters made sense because it was God testing us.

In Voltaire's witty classic novel *Candide* (which was published in 1759), the hero, a young man called Candide, suffers all sorts of disasters. Each time something terrible happens, Candide's philosopher companion, Dr Pangloss, ludicrously defends God. Always Dr Pangloss insists God is not cruelly punishing or peevishly testing us. Always in a disaster there is sense, purpose and a greater good.

Voltaire derided such ideas. His message was that there was inexcusable evil in the world. In Voltaire's view, we know nothing, we are ignorant creatures and God is silent. The best we could do is live in doubt and uncertain hope.

Who are you to question God?

The doubts of people like Voltaire have been countered by asking, 'Who are you to doubt God?' We do not understand why God allows an earthquake to destroy Lisbon, but, whatever it was, surely God has a good reason. Who are we, after all, to question God? Only God really sees the big picture. As al-Ghazali wrote, 'A really pious man always feels that whatever evil has happened to him it is for his benefit.'

'Where were you when I laid the earth's foundations?' Job 38:4

In the Bible story of Job, God tests Job with many disasters. When Job protests that he is badly treated, God answers by telling him that, compared to God, Job is ignorant of the world and he does not have the right to question God.

The claim that we cannot see the big picture and do not have the right to question God has been developed into what is sometimes called the **aesthetic argument**. Aesthetics is about beauty and art.

The Greek philosopher Plotinus was one of the earliest of thinkers to come up with an aesthetic argument. Plotinus lived two hundred years after Jesus died. A further two hundred years later, St Augustine, who deeply admired Plotinus' work, also used a very similar aesthetic argument.

Plotinus (205–70CE)

'We are like people ignorant of painting who complain that the colours are not beautiful everywhere in the picture.'

The aesthetic argument

Look at the painting below on the left. You might think, 'This is a pretty ordinary or even ugly painting.' You might think the colours are not very beautiful or the lines do not make sense. But if you step back and see the whole picture, (see the painting on the right), you might say, 'Wow…what a beautiful picture!'

We are like people ignorant of the painting as a whole. We see evil and ugly things happening in the world – an earthquake here, a road accident there – and we conclude that evil in the world makes no sense and is inexcusable. But if we could see what God sees, if we could see the whole picture, things would look very different. Taken as a whole, the black and the shadow parts in the picture are not ugly. The dark parts provide the contrast with the light parts so that, taken as a whole, the picture is beautiful.

This helps us understand how we see the world. Although parts of the world may seem evil, if we could see the big picture, we would see that these things are not evil but are a necessary part of what makes the world a good and harmonious whole.

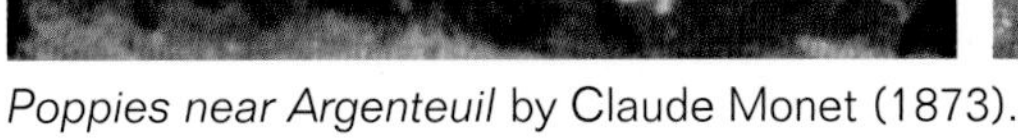

Poppies near Argenteuil by Claude Monet (1873).

The big picture argument

Something like the aesthetic argument is also found in Islam. If you look at one small part of the universe, it may look like a tangled mess. A violent typhoon, or the death of a child by disease, may seem like a pointless or evil event. But if you could see the big picture, you would see that everything makes sense. There is a pattern in the whole universe. In much the same way as Islamic decorative art viewed close up would seem like a senseless mess, but if we could see the big picture, we would see a harmony and a pattern to it all.

Islamic decorative art

We may see the world as a tangled mess but God has planned the universe as a harmonious whole.

The idea that what we see may seem evil, but that if we could see the big picture we would know better, is found in a story in the Qur'an (Surah 18:67–83). The story tells of a meeting between Moses and a mysterious wise man. The wise man is not named in the Qur'an, but traditionally he is called Khandir. Below is a shortened version of the story.

The story of Moses and Khandir

Khandir knew the ways of the Lord. One day Moses said to him, 'Khandir, you are a man of great wisdom, I wish to be with you so that I might learn more.' Khandir allowed Moses to follow him but Khandir warned Moses that he must not question anything that he should do. Khandir said to Moses, 'You must bear patiently and not question anything I do until I myself mention it.'

The two men walked on together to a river. After a while a boat came by and the kindly captain ordered his crew to pick them up. As they went down the river Moses was shocked. Khandir had punctured a hole in the bottom of the boat. No one else on board had seen the

The kindly captain picked them up.

damage Khandir had done or had noticed the water slowly seeping into the boat. At last the boat arrived close to a city. Moses and Khandir thanked the captain and the crew and got off the boat.

As the boat continued on its journey Moses could contain himself no longer. 'Did you put a hole in the boat so that it would sink and drown the crew and passengers on board? What you have done was a dreadful thing.' Khandir looked at Moses and said, 'Did I not tell you that you must not question anything I do?' Moses' mind was very troubled, but the two men continued their journey together.

At last they arrived at the city. Moses and Khandir asked the people of the city for a little food but the people turned them away. As they were leaving, Khandir saw a wall that was about to collapse. Khandir laboured hard, carefully taking each stone and resetting it so that the wall was strong and well repaired.

Moses was baffled. 'What is it you are doing, Khandir? You have laboured long hours repairing that wall. We are hungry and you could have taken payment for such hard work.'

'You have questioned me again,' said Khandir, 'and now we must part. But before we do I will tell you the truth of that which you could not bear patiently. The boat belonged to poor men. Following the boat was a king who, had the boat been undamaged, would have seized the vessel and would have brutally murdered the captain, the crew and all the passengers. Underneath the wall I repaired there was a treasure that belonged to two orphaned boys. Had the wall collapsed the two boys would have lost their treasure and suffered poverty all their lives.'

He laboured hard so that the wall was strong and well repaired.

Moses lowered his head and nodded for he knew that this day he had gained a little in wisdom.

St Irenaeus (130–202CE)

'Now it was necessary that man should in the first instance be created; and having been created, should receive growth...'

The soul-making argument – Irenaeus

The soul-making argument has been around for a long time. Irenaeus was one of the first Christian thinkers to suggest the idea. St Irenaeus lived over eighteen hundred years ago. In his book *Against Heresies*, Irenaeus suggested that when God first created humans, God made us special with human souls. However, in those early days, our souls were immature and only at the start of growing and developing. By living in the world our souls would grow and strengthen. Finally, some time in the future, our souls would achieve the glorious state of maturity God had intended for us.

Only when our souls had grown and matured would we truly know perfection and God. Irenaeus said that we were created in the 'image' of God, but finally we would achieve our perfected state and become in the 'likeness' of God.

In the twentieth century, the person most associated with the soul-making argument is John Hick, a British professor of philosophy. John Hick's argument goes something like this.

John Hick (1922–)

'Is this the kind of world that God might make as an environment in which moral beings may be fashioned...into "children of God"?'

The soul-making argument – John Hick

God is not like a caring pet owner. God has not placed humans in a giant pet cage and tried to make life for humans as pleasant as possible by giving us food, water, warmth and toys to play with. This world is not meant to be a perfect pet cage. Instead, this world is one in which we will inevitably experience hardships, difficulties and challenges.

We have to face up to suffering and challenges and by doing so this helps to make us stronger. Dealing with problems and disasters help build character and strength of mind. Only when things go wrong do we grow stronger and in time become better people.

If the world was perfect and nothing went wrong, we would never have to show or develop these qualities. Instead, like immature children, we could laugh our way through life. Everything would be a trivial game as nothing would go wrong and there would be no serious outcomes.

By experiencing the challenges of this world, we become spiritually grown-up and so more like the final adult spiritual being God ultimately wants us to become.

As the poet John Keats wrote in a letter to his brother and sister in 1819, this is a 'vale of soul-making', a world of pains and troubles 'to school an intelligence and make it a soul'.

How can suffering really bring about growth? Jesus' well-known story of a young man who leaves home and tries to make it on his own may be seen as a story of how a person can change from being spiritually immature to being spiritually grown-up. Here is one way in which the story may be told.

John Keats (1795–1827)

'Do you not see how necessary a world of pains and troubles is to school an intelligence and make it a soul?'

The boy who grew up

One day a younger man tells his father that he wants to leave home and try and make it in the big world.

The father knows that it is a dangerous world out there and does not want him to go. Nevertheless, the young man thinks he knows best and is not prepared to listen. The young man leaves home with the money that is due to him. It is not long before things go badly wrong. The young man wastes his money and is soon abandoned by his so-called friends. Over the years he suffers famine and poverty. He tries to get a job but the only work available is degrading.

'...the younger son got together all he had, set off for a distant country.' Luke 15:13

Eventually, he decides to return home. But the young man that returns home is very different from the boy who left. He has grown up. Through hardship, setbacks and disasters he has matured. He is no longer the brash, over-confident, irresponsible boy who left all that time ago. He has experienced the hardship of life and although it was painful it has made him into a much better person. He can admit his weaknesses, he knows the dangers of trying to get rich quick, and he knows the value of hard work.

Unit 7 Things to do

Activity 1 Pyramid – can the problem of evil be answered?

Arrange the six triangles below into a pyramid with the view you agree with most at the top of the pyramid, your second and third choice underneath, and the three views you least agree with at the base. If you do not agree, talk about why. Give a reason for your first choice. If you do not really agree with any of these views, write a triangle of your own.

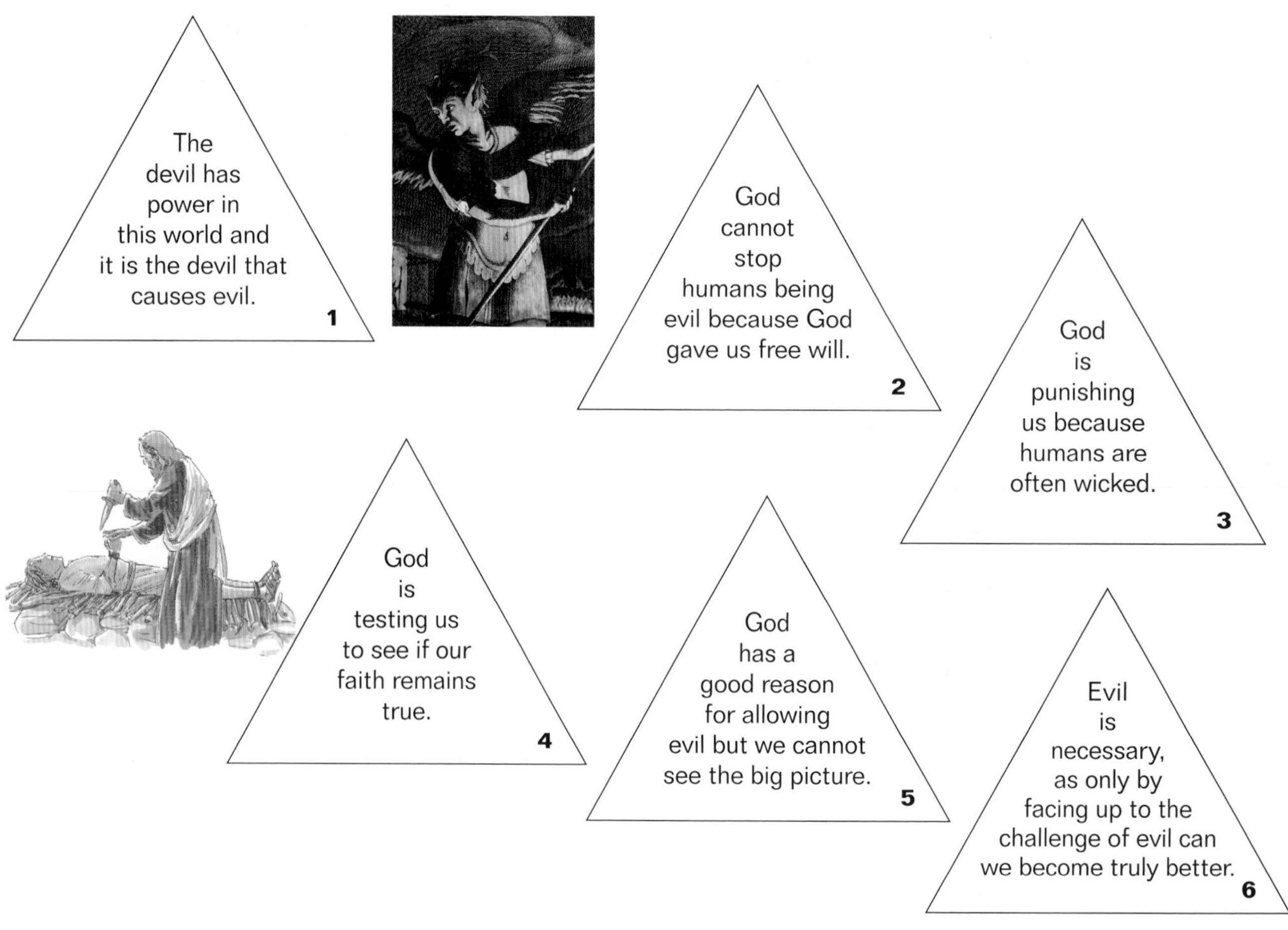

Activity 2 Research survey – why is there evil in the world?

a Survey the views of your friends and relatives, asking the question, 'Why is there evil in the world?'

b Make a record of each person's response.

- Can their answers be grouped under any common headings?
- Draw up a bar chart to show the results of your survey.
- What conclusions do you think you can draw from your survey?

Evil visited us, we don't know why, says head

Activity 3 Useful words

In the boxes below are three words. What do these words mean? Which of these words would best finish the sentences below? Make up a sentence of your own using one of these words.

omnipotent **spiritual** **aesthetic**

Nothing seemed to dislodge her sense of inner tranquillity and I knew I was in the presence of a person who was deeply...

While listening to music, I sometimes marvel at its beauty and I wonder why we have a sense of the...

God is in full control of this world. God is not just powerful. God is...

Activity 4 A class discussion

Geoff, Amina and Linda discuss their ideas about God and evil.

Can you find any examples of:

a disrespectful or emotive language

b anecdotal evidence

c using analogy

d use being made of respectful language or a moderate tone.

Geoff When you look at how much evil there is in the world, it is obvious to anyone with only half a brain that God has made a right mess of things.

Amina I understand why you might think that, but I cannot agree with you. I think we are like passengers on board a train. Some of the passengers are ripping up the seats and being evil. But God is in charge because God is driving the train.

Linda That is an idea worth thinking about, but I have my doubts. What about living things that kill us, like the flu virus? If God made all living things, why did God make the flu virus?

Amina — You cannot blame God for everything. My grandfather died of flu but that was because he never rested when he should have done. So often people die because they do not look after themselves.

Geoff — Of course God is to blame. If you cannot see that, you must be a bit of a dummy. If there is a God, which I doubt, then God is just sitting back and doing nothing while innocent people suffer.

Linda — I do not agree with that although I know believing in God can be hard. I think we are a bit like ants crawling around. An ant does not know what the President of America is thinking so we do not really know what God is thinking or what God is up to.

One of the three is not making much of an effort to use respectful language. Suggest some improvements.

Activity 5 A class debate

Organise a formal class debate. In teams of four, choose a motion to debate: you could use one of the motions suggested below or develop a new motion of your own. You need one team proposing and one team opposing each motion. Suggest a time for any one speaker of between one to two minutes.

This house believes:

a In a world in which billions of innocent people suffer, it makes little sense claiming that there is a good and all-powerful God.

b It cannot be denied that evil things happen in this world, but also it cannot be denied that there is a good and loving God.

c Religion is a waste of time; we should just get on and make the world a better place.

d Atheists and sceptics should be invited to speak on Radio 4's *Thought for the Day*, not just religious believers.

Unit 8

Is belief in God reasonable?

We have seen how the various arguments about God have been bounced backwards and forwards over many hundreds of years. Why has this argument not been settled once and for all? Why do atheists and theists disagree?

The Cambridge philosopher John Wisdom (in an essay he wrote in 1944 called 'Gods') had a go at trying to explain why they disagree. John Wisdom suggested that part of the answer might be found in the following story.

The parable of the gardener

After being away for a long period of time, two friends return home. They go outside and walk about their neglected garden. As they walk about, they notice that the grass is overgrown, there are weeds coming up through the pathway and there are many leaves scattered about the place. But, surprisingly, they also notice that a few of the plants look really strong and healthy.

'Two friends return to their long neglected garden…' John Wisdom

One friend says to the other, 'It must be that a gardener has been coming and doing something about these plants.' The other friend says, 'No, I don't think so. There is no gardener, this garden has just been neglected.'

They ask the neighbours, but no one has seen anyone at work in the garden. The first friend says, 'Look at the way these plants are arranged. They are not just scattered about. They have been planted with thought and care. There must be a gardener that has been coming in and working on this garden.'

The two friends examine the garden very carefully. Sometimes they come upon things that suggest that a gardener has been at work. For example, the ivy looks as if it has been cut back; between the plants there are hardly any weeds. But sometimes they come upon things that suggest that no gardener has been at work. For example, there are several holes in the fence that have not been repaired; bindweed is covering many of the trees.

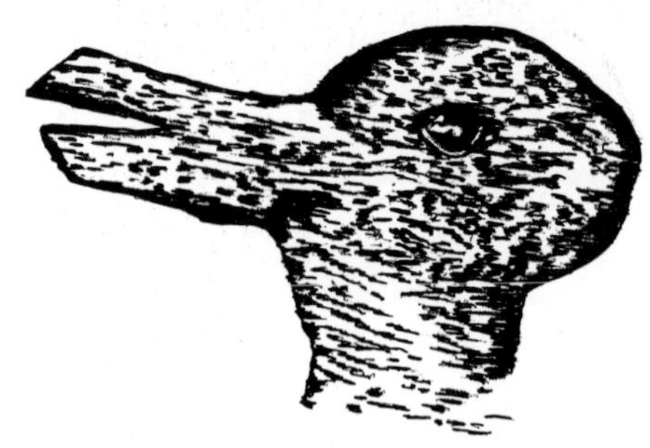

If you examine this picture carefully, what can you see? Is there more than one answer?

After all this careful checking, the first friend still says, 'I still believe a gardener comes,' while the other says, 'I don't believe there is a gardener.'

Two reasonable answers

What do we learn from this story? Does it help us understand arguments about God?

The two friends looking at the same garden arrive at two quite different answers. Although they arrive at opposite conclusions, the two answers seem perfectly reasonable. The answer that 'There is a gardener' and the answer that 'There is no gardener' are both reasonable answers. They arrive at different answers and yet neither of them is being blind, superstitious or ridiculous. They both see the same garden but their **perception** of the garden is quite different.

Two reasonable answers? What can you see in this picture? Are there two answers, both of which are reasonable?

John Wisdom asks: is the same sort of thing happening when people argue about God? Theists are not superstitious and atheists are not blind. The argument is not about facts. Both atheists and theists see the same things in the world – beauty, order, goodness and evil. But their perception of these things leads to two different answers, in much the same way as two people looking at the same image. In the image opposite one person might see a young lady and another might see an old woman. Yet both answers are reasonable; both answers are rational.

In the image opposite of the 'young lady and the old woman', both answers are reasonable and both answers are true. But in 'The parable of the gardener' both answers cannot be true. There cannot 'be a gardener' and 'not be a gardener'. The same is true about the argument about God. There cannot 'be a God' and 'not be a God'. But looking at the world around us, using what evidence we have, is the belief in God reasonable?

Is belief reasonable?

Earlier we learnt that philosophers believed that their arguments for God proved that there is a God. Aquinas, for example, believed that his cosmological argument proved that there is a God. William Paley believed that his design argument proved that there is a God.

Richard Swinburne (1934–)

'The case for the existence of God is a cumulative one.'

They believed that their proof resembled the way in which Euclid had proved that the interior angles of a triangle are equal to two right angles. They believed they had provided what is called a **deductive** proof. In his 1979 book, *The Existence of God*, Professor Richard Swinburne gives the following example of a deductive proof.

Premise 1: No material bodies travel faster than light.
Premise 2: My car is a material body.
Conclusion: My car does not travel faster than light.

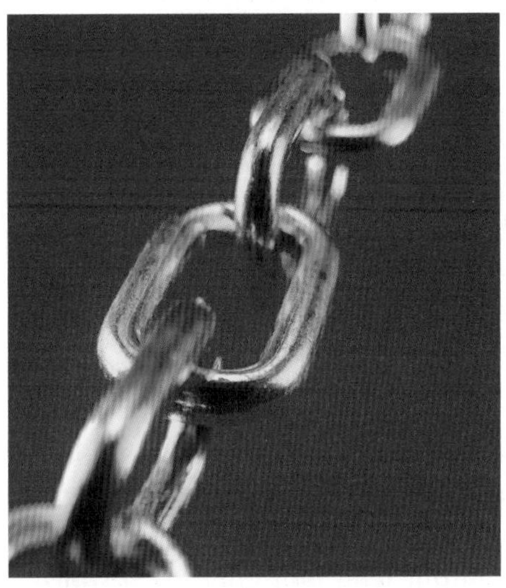

Premise 1: A gardener grows plants.

Premise 2: Sam Gamgee is a gardener.

Conclusion: Sam Gamgee grows plants.

A deductive proof is like a logical chain of reasoning. If you accept the first two links in the chain, premise 1 and premise 2, then you must also accept the conclusion.

Richard Swinburne does not try to prove God using a deductive argument. He is less ambitious. Instead, he hopes to show that the belief in God is **reasonable**. This is like the friend in 'The parable of the gardener' who believes in a gardener. The friend knows that pointing out the strong and healthy plants and the well-trimmed ivy does not prove there is a gardener. But it does enable him to say, 'My belief in a gardener is not ridiculous, it is reasonable.' Proving that there is a God using deduction may be impossible. But it may be possible to show that the belief in God is reasonable.

Richard Swinburne argues that it is reasonable to believe in God, but the case for God is not based on one argument but on many arguments that should be taken together. In his book *The Existence of God,* Richard Swinburne presents what he calls his **cumulative** case for God. This is roughly what he says:

The cumulative case for God

Many of the arguments for God have the same pattern. Arguments for God usually begin by pointing out 'something' in the universe that we can all see and agree upon. It is then claimed that this 'something' is puzzling. This 'something', however, might well be expected if there is a God. As this 'something' is there for all of us to see, it makes it reasonable for us to believe there is a God.

The 'something' could be very large, like the existence of the universe, or it might be something smaller, like order in the universe. Or it might be something that is a lot smaller, like a religious experience that you have had personally.

Each of these arguments, like the cosmological argument, or the design argument, or the religious experience argument, on its own might not be entirely convincing. But if you put all these arguments together, they mount up and make a strong case.

The Safecracker case

Suppose, for example, you suspected that a man with a reputation for robbing banks, Johnny Safecracker, had robbed a local bank. As part of the case you might discover Johnny had in his house a large number of bank notes. Although this is suspicious, it does not prove Johnny is a thief. Later, a witness identifies Johnny as the person she saw hanging around the bank late at night. Later still, you discover Johnny's fingerprints are on the safe. Soon after that you learn that a button, which was found close to the bank's vault, matches a button missing from one of Johnny's jackets.

Each of these four bits of evidence might not on their own prove Johnny had committed the crime. But if you add all the evidence together, it is reasonable to believe Johnny is guilty of the robbery.

The leaky bucket argument

Professor Antony Flew, for most of his life, has been sceptical of the arguments for God. He has suggested the idea that each argument mounts up like evidence to provide a reasonable case for God is unlikely.

Antony Flew (1923–)

'...the ten-leaky-buckets-tactic, applied to arguments, none of which hold water...'

In his 1966 book *God and Philosophy*, Antony Flew says that there is a difference in the way in which evidence can be built up and may be used to make a case. The building up of good evidence is valid. But it is not valid to put together several arguments for God, each one of which is mistaken. Claiming that several unsound arguments add up to make a sound case does not work.

If each argument for God is flawed, then each argument is like a bucket that leaks. Instead of holding water and providing a case for God, every one of them is holed and simply leaks water. Adding them together does not make a watertight case for God. Instead, all you have got is a collection of leaky buckets.

Very recently, Flew has changed his mind about God. He does not believe in a Christian God but he does now believe that some sort of super-intelligence must have been involved in the origin of life.

Questions of great consequence

Joseph Butler (1692–1752)

'...in questions of great consequence, a reasonable man will think it concerns him to remark lower probabilities...'

In 1736 a Church of England priest impressed many people with his book *The Analogy of Religion, Natural and Revealed, to the Constitution and Concern of Nature*. The author was Joseph Butler. Usually the book is more simply called, *Butler's Analogy*.

One of Joseph Butler's main ideas was that when it comes to really important questions we often make up our minds even though we may not have much evidence.

Deciding if there is a God is a really important question. After all, if you do not believe in God, it could make a real difference when you die. Belief in God could mean paradise or damnation. As believing that there is a God is a serious question, it is right to make up our minds even though the evidence may not be that good.

Take, for example, the following situation:

Saving your brother

You are crossing a bridge with your younger brother. Part of the bridge collapses and your brother falls into the water. Suddenly you have to face a question of great consequence. Are you going to stand by and watch your brother drown? Or are you going to jump in and try and save him?

Quickly weighing up the situation, you might be short of good evidence to be certain what to do. The current in the water might be a lot stronger than you think. The water might be so freezing that both of you could drown. You have not got all the evidence you would like to make a reasonable judgement. Nevertheless, even though the evidence may not be good, many older sisters or brothers would still jump in and do their best.

Or let us take another case. This example comes from an American writer, James Kiefer.

Cyanide in the coffee

You are sitting with a friend in a science lab. You put some sugar into your nice cup of coffee and are about to have a sip. Your friend calls out, 'Stop! Don't drink that coffee. I was watching and it was not sugar you put in your coffee, it was cyanide poison!' You look down and sure enough in front of you there is a jar of sugar and a jar of cyanide.

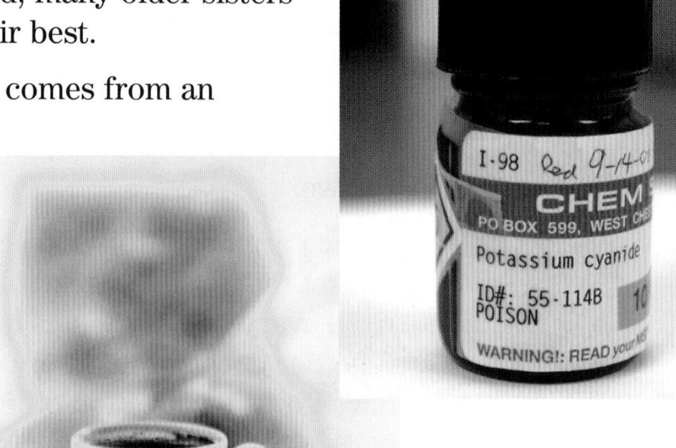

You are now not quite sure which jar you dipped your spoon into. Was it the sugar, as you thought, or was it the cyanide? You sniff your coffee but you cannot detect any cyanide. Your friend thinks you put cyanide into your coffee but he admits he could have made a mistake. Even though the evidence is not certain, are you going to risk it and drink your coffee? It is not very likely, is it?

The point Joseph Butler is making is this: sceptics who refuse to believe in God on the grounds that the evidence is not good enough are not taking into account the great consequence of the question they are facing. Given how serious the question is, even though the evidence may not be perfect, believing in God is reasonable.

What is religion?

Most of this book has been about religious ideas and arguments. It has looked at what people believe and the reasons they have given for why they believe. But are people religious because of reasons? This might seem like an odd question to ask. But we know that a lot of what we humans say, do and believe does not come from reasons. Let us look at some examples.

Why do people smoke? Smoking cigarettes is expensive, very unhealthy and they do kill. Viewed rationally, there are no good reasons for smoking, and yet people carry on smoking.

Or what about falling in love? When a person falls in love we would think it a little odd if they sat down and made out a list of reasons for or against falling in love. Falling in love is not something you decide to do based on a list of reasons. Falling in love hits you like an inner necessity. When it happens, it is something you cannot deny, it just happens.

'Religious essence is neither thinking nor acting, but intuition and feeling.' Friedrich Schleiermacher

Friedrich Schleiermacher was one of the most brilliant of Christian thinkers. He really made people think about what religion actually is, and today he is widely seen as a modern pioneer of thinking about religion. His name has come up briefly before when we looked at the question, 'Who made the devil?' (See p. 71)

In one of his best-known books, *On Religion: Speeches to its Cultured Despisers* (published in 1799), Friedrich Schleiermacher wrote about religion in a very new way. Schleiermacher said that religion was an **inner necessity**. It was a feeling that cannot be denied. This is what he said.

An inner necessity

There are many clever people today who are sceptical about religion. They think of religion as being two things. First, they see it as a set of beliefs. Second, they see religion as being rules about right and wrong. In other words, they think being religious is about believing in certain things and behaving in a way that is good. This is a distorted view of religion.

Religion is not a rational decision a person makes about what they should believe in or how they should behave. A person is not religious because one day they sit down and weigh up a series of beliefs – like God, life after death, miracles – and decide they will believe in these things. Religion is not something you accept because of reasons.

Religion comes from an inner necessity. People who believe in God believe because they must. It comes out of a personal encounter, an intuition, a feeling. Religious belief happens in a person not because of so-called proofs. It happens when there is a sort of inner ignition of love of the Most High. When this happens, a person becomes aware that they must live not a common life but must strive for something much higher.

Inside all of us there is a deep awareness of the Most High, an awareness of God. All religions try to put into words this deep awareness. Although this inner feeling in some people is covered over, it is there within all of us. And it is this inner feeling which, when we are alive to it, shouts out at us and tells us, 'There is a God.'

'...you cannot believe in him by force of will or because you want to use him for solace and help, but because you must.' Friedrich Schleiermacher

The last word?

Friedrich Schleiermacher might well have got people to think about the importance of feelings when it comes to having a religious life. But Schleiermacher was not the last word on the subject. People still continue to discuss whether religious beliefs are true or not. Philosophy of religion is still going on. There are plenty of people suggesting new ideas and developing new arguments. They try to learn from the past, avoiding errors others have made, picking up leads and trying to edge towards a better idea of what is true.

Philosophy does help us to think about things so we can avoid using contradictions or being inconsistent.

Philosophy may not always provide us with a clear right or wrong answer. What it does, however, is just as important. It sharpens our thinking and helps us to see our errors. It does help us to get across our ideas. And it does help us think about things so we can avoid using contradictions, or being inconsistent or sloppy in our thinking.

And finally…

Who's who?

al-Ghazali (1058–1111)

Born in what is now Iran, al-Ghazali became a professor at one of the great centres for Muslim learning, the University of Baghdad. After a few years, he gave up his job and became a wandering holy man. He wrote many books in which he claimed that Muslim rituals like prayer and fasting are important but he emphasised their spiritual value.

Aquinas, St Thomas (c.1225–74)

Born in Italy, St Thomas Aquinas is, for some, one of the most admired of all Christian thinkers. Often called the 'Doctor of the Church', his influence, particularly in the Catholic Church, has been enormous. Aquinas was influenced by the great Greek philosopher Aristotle. Aquinas developed the cosmological argument. A version of this argument is called 'the first cause argument'.

Augustine of Hippo, St (354–430CE)

St Augustine was born in North Africa. His ideas helped shape Christianity early in its history. He is known as the 'Father of the Church'. Augustine used ideas that were first developed by Greek philosophers like Plato and Plotinus. Augustine argued that God made a world that was good and that evil came into the world mainly because of Adam and Eve.

Bacon, Francis (1561–1626)

Francis Bacon was a British politician who served Queen Elizabeth I and King James I. He eventually became the Lord Chancellor of England. He achieved fame in literature, the law and science, as well as philosophy. He developed what he called in Latin the *Novum Organum* or *The New Instrument.* This was a way of gaining knowledge based on observations while avoiding errors and mistakes.

Butler, Joseph (1692–1752)

Joseph Butler joined the Church of England as a young man. He rose up through the ranks of the Church to become the Bishop of Durham. The fear of death and the hope for a life after death formed an important part of his philosophy. In his day, his work was much admired even by those who disagreed with his ideas.

Darwin, Charles (1809–82)

Charles Darwin developed the theory that life evolved by natural selection. This idea has become accepted by almost all biologists. It remains the key idea to explain life around us. When he was a young man, Darwin believed in God, but it is thought his faith was shattered when his daughter Annie died.

Dunbar, Helen Flanders (1902–59)

Born in Chicago in America, Helen Dunbar was a pioneer in psychosomatic medicine. She was interested in both religion and science. As a medical doctor in the early 1930s, she carried out a major study into how closely emotion and illness went together. In 1938, she established the first journal of psychosomatic medicine, which reported on the latest research on how the mind and body influenced each other.

Euclid of Alexandria (325–265BCE)

Little is known about Euclid's life other than he taught in the city of Alexandria, in Egypt. He is the best known of ancient mathematicians and his book, *The Elements*, has become a classic. The book begins with certain definitions and five statements or postulates which appear to be irrefutable. Using these definitions and postulates, Euclid is able to build a large system of mathematical proofs.

Flew, Antony (1923–)

Professor Antony Flew is one of Britain's leading philosophers. For most of his life he has been an atheist, although now, at the age of 81, Flew has said he is best labelled a deist. Many of his early books have been very critical of religious arguments. He has argued that it is a problem for those with a religious belief if they cannot admit any circumstances in which the belief in God would be shown to be wrong.

Francis of Assisi, St (1182–1226)

Born into a wealthy family, Francis had a call from God to give up all wealth and luxury. He adopted a life of prayer, humility, poverty and service to the poor. He founded an order of friars called the Franciscans. As well as a love of God and a simple life, he showed a love of animals and nature.

Freud, Sigmund (1856–1939)

Sigmund Freud is generally recognised as being the founder of psychoanalysis. He was one of the most important thinkers of the twentieth century. He developed the idea that much of our behaviour and feelings are due to hidden reasons in the mind. Freud called the hidden part of the mind 'the unconscious'. Freud believed that religious faith was an illusion created by our childlike wish for a protective father figure.

Hardy, Alister (1896–1985)

The distinguished scientist Sir Alister Hardy was a Professor of Zoology. He pioneered the science of marine biology. His interest in religion also led him to set up The Religious Experience Research Centre. Members of the population were invited to describe any spiritual or religious experience they may have had. Hardy discovered that there are many people who claim to have felt a presence or power but that these people rarely talk about their experiences.

Hick, John (1922–)

Born in Yorkshire, John Hick is one of Britain's leading philosophers of religion. He was a conscientious objector during World War II. After the war he became a Christian minister. His book, *Evil and the God of Love*, provided a detailed discussion of the problem of evil. He has also pioneered ideas on how Christianity and the other great faiths can view each other with respect and learn from each other.

Hume, David (1711–76)

The Scottish thinker David Hume was one of the greatest of all sceptical philosophers. Some were shocked by his criticism of religious claims, believing him to be irreligious. However, others found him to be a man full of wisdom and charm. Hume played a major part in developing the British empirical tradition, arguing that it is only from experience that we acquire knowledge of things.

Irenaeus (130–202CE)

St Irenaeus was probably born in Smyrna, in what is today called Turkey. He became the Bishop of Lyons in France. Irenaeus claimed that humans were created in the 'image of God' and that humans have not yet been brought into their final 'likeness of God'. His ideas about spiritual growth, that humans are moving towards a higher state, begins to answer, for some, the question, 'Why is there evil and suffering in the world?'

James, William (1842–1910)

William James was born into an affluent American family in New York. His younger brother Henry became a famous novelist. William studied the new science of psychology. His interest in religion and his knowledge of psychology resulted in his book *The Varieties of Religious Experience*. James believed that the 'ideal religion' forces itself into the world, causing experiences like prayer and visions.

Kant, Immanuel (1724–1804)

Immanuel Kant is often considered to be one of the greatest of modern philosophers. He spent his whole life in or near the East Prussian city of Königsberg. His life was extremely regular! Kant said that reason could neither prove nor disprove that there is a God. Kant, however, did believe in God. He thought that in order to live a moral life it is necessary to suppose that there is a God.

Leibniz, Gottfried (1646–1716)

Born in Leipzig, in Germany, Gottfried Leibniz travelled widely across Europe. He was a brilliant mathematician. He wrote a number of arguments that he believed proved there was a God. He also wrote a book called *Theodicy* in which he believed he had provided an answer to the problem of evil. He argued that evil is a necessary part of the world.

Mill, John Stuart (1806–73)

The British philosopher John Stuart Mill is probably best known for his belief that what is viewed as right or wrong should be based on whatever gives the greatest happiness to the greatest number of people. Mill was an atheist, but he firmly believed that even though there was no God there clearly was right and wrong. He also wrote about liberty and the importance of freedom.

Newman, John Henry (1801–90)

John Henry Newman was born in London. By the age of twenty-four he was a minister in the Church of England. Some twenty years later he left the Church of England and became a Roman Catholic priest. He was deeply opposed to the view that there is no truth in religion and that 'one greed is as good as another'. To Newman, our conscience came from God and was a demonstration of God working inside of us.

Paine, Thomas (1737–1809)

Thomas Paine was born in England, the son of Quaker parents. He went to live in America when he was about 37 and played an important part in the American War of Independence. He was very critical of the Bible, but was a deist, not an atheist. He wrote, 'I believe in one God…and I hope for happiness beyond this life.' He opposed slavery and suggested that there should be a world peace organisation.

Paley, William (1743–1805)

William Paley was a priest in the Church of England. Paley wrote several very influential books on philosophy and Christianity. His book, *A View of the Evidence of Christianity*, was required reading at Cambridge University for over a hundred years. His design argument, with its image of God as an intelligent watchmaker, continues to give rise to a great deal of discussion.

Plotinus (205–270CE)

Plotinus was born in Egypt and for a while he studied in the city of Alexandria. Eventually he settled down in Rome. Plotinus deeply admired the work of the great Greek philosopher Plato. St Augustine described Plato's ideas as 'the most pure and bright in all philosophy' and of Plotinus he said he was the man in whom 'Plato lived again'. Although not a Christian himself, Plotinus' influence on Christianity has been great.

Rashdall, Hastings (1858–1924)

Hastings Rashdall was an English philosopher and a minister in the Church of England. He wrote many books, some of which were about the Christian faith, but he also wrote about the idea of good and evil more generally. He argued that we have a clear knowledge of right and wrong, and that this demonstrated that there was a God who was the source of our clear knowledge.

Russell, Bertrand (1872–1970)

Betrand Russell was born into an aristocratic family. His grandfather was Prime Minister. He once said of himself, 'I ought to call myself an agnostic; but, for all practical purposes, I am an athiest.' Bertrand Russell was an outspoken critic of religion. He believed that religion in the main had been harmful and was the source of a great deal of intolerance and violence.

Schleiermacher, Friedrich (1768–1834)

Friedrich Schleiermacher was born in what is now a part of Poland. He studied in Berlin and became a Christian minister. Schleiermacher said that religion was not a set of beliefs or rituals. Nor was religion a set of rules about right or wrong. The essence of religion, for Schleiermacher, was the feeling of absolute dependence. Belief was not a rational decision but an 'irresistible necessity'.

Soubirous, Bernadette (1844–79)

St Bernadette Soubirous was born in the village of Lourdes in southern France. At the age of fourteen she experienced eighteen visions of the Virgin Mary. Her experience resulted in Lourdes becoming a major centre for Christian pilgrimage. Many apparent miracles have happened at Lourdes, 66 of which have been officially recognised by the Catholic Church.

Spinoza, Benedict (1632–77)

Benedict Spinoza was born in Holland in the city of Amsterdam. His parents were Jewish. Although brought up as a Jew, Spinoza did not believe in the God as described by Judaism or by Christianity. He believed that by starting with self-evident truths it was possible to prove that logically there was a God just as it is logically true that if you add 3 and 2, you would have 5.

Swinburne, Richard (1934–)

Richard Swinburne is a British philosopher who has been a professor at Keele and at Oxford University. He has consistently defended the belief in God, claiming that the belief in God is rational and makes clear sense. For Richard Swinburne, the idea of God helps us to make sense of why there is a world. Also, the idea of God helps us to understand why animals and humans have evolved.

Tindall, Matthew (1655–1733)

Matthew Tindall taught at Oxford University. His book, *Christianity as Old as the Creation*, became a standard textbook of deism. Matthew Tindall believed that the basic teachings of Jesus are true but that Church leaders had added many beliefs and practices that did not come from Jesus and were not essential to Christianity. For example, Tindall did not believe in hell or the miracles of Jesus.

Voltaire (1694–1778)

At the age of twenty-one, the French philosopher Voltaire was imprisoned for making fun of the king. At the age of 32, he was forced into exile. Voltaire was very critical of what he saw as hypocrisy in the Catholic Church. However, he did believe in God. Nearly 60 years before William Paley he wrote, 'I shall always be convinced that a watch proves a watchmaker, and that a universe proves a God.'

Wilson, Edward (1929–)

Dr Edward Wilson is regarded as one of the most important zoologists of the twenty-first century. He is a Professor of Biology at Harvard University and is recognised as probably the world's leading authority on ants. With his theory of socio-biology, Edward Wilson claimed that social animals, like humans, generally behave according to rules that have evolved over a long period of time.

Wisdom, John (1904–93)

John Wisdom was a British philosopher, working in Cambridge and then America. He was influenced by the philosophy of Ludwig Wittgenstein. He helped develop the idea that in a discussion about religion truth may come as disclosure, that is, suddenly seeing something you have always known about in a new light.

Woolston, Thomas (1669–1733)

Thomas Woolston studied at Cambridge University. His study of the Bible convinced him that the miracles of the New Testament, in particular, were not true. His book was one of the first to raise doubts about the resurrection of Jesus and other miracles. His ideas got him into trouble. Instead of being taken seriously, he was dismissed as being mad. For his views he was ridiculed, fined and imprisoned.

Zoroaster (Zarathustra) (628– 551 BCE)

Zoroaster is believed to have been born in a part of Persia that is modern-day Azerbaijan. Often known as 'the Persian Prophet', Zoroaster was the founder of Zoroastrianism. Following a vision from the God of Light, he believed he had been given a mission to preach. He taught that there was a war taking place between the God of Light and the God of Evil. Zoroastrianism has largely died out in the Middle East but it continues to survive in India as the Parsi religion.

The useful word list

aesthetic

This word is about understanding what makes something beautiful. If a person thinks about what makes a painting beautiful, this could be called 'exploring its aesthetic'.

agnostic

A person who believes in **agnosticism**. An agnostic holds the view that it is not very likely that there is a God. This view might be held on the grounds that there is not enough **evidence**. Or an agnostic might say that the existence of God is very unlikely but there is always a possibility that there may be a God.

agnosticism

Agnosticism is the view that it is not very likely that there is a God. Agnosticism does not claim that there definitely cannot be a God. It claims that it is possible and it would be wrong to close one's mind to the possibility.

altruism

Is the view that life should be lived to the highest possible standard of goodness, which is beyond normal expectations. Altruism is a life based on only the purest of motives.

altruistic

Living life according to the principle of **altruism**. An altruistic person does good things that may involve a great deal of personal sacrifice. They may do good but receive nothing back, and expect nothing back, that would benefit them personally.

analogy

An analogy compares two things and a similarity between them is suggested. An analogy may be used to make an argument clearer or more vivid. Usually an analogy suggests a similarity between something known and something new and unknown.

anecdotal

A reference to a single event or incidence. If an anecdote is used as **evidence** to support an argument, it is a form of **generalising from the particular**. Being a single event, an anecdote is unlikely to provide enough evidence to make a valid **conclusion**.

assumption

An assumption is something taken for granted. An assumption is often the cause of flawed thinking. Often a person is unaware that they have made an assumption. When this happens, it is called a **hidden assumption**.

atheism

The belief that there is no God.

atheist

A person who does not believe in God. Or, to put it in a way many atheists would prefer, an atheist asserts that there is no God. An atheist may be hostile to religion. Or an atheist may be indifferent to religion, believing it to be merely an illusion or a fiction.

ayats

An ayat is an Arabic word that is used a lot in the **Qur'an**. It refers to things that can be seen around us that are believed to be signs of God. Usually these signs are natural events and are seen as being so extraordinary or so well ordered that they point to the existence of God.

benevolent

A word that is used to describe a person who is kind, generous or charitable. The word is often used to describe a loving, kind and forgiving God.

conclusion

A final statement or point of view usually arrived at after considering the evidence. A conclusion may be a **logical** conclusion based on earlier statements. Statements that lead to a logical conclusion are called **premises**.

conscience

A word to describe a feeling of knowing right from wrong. Conscience is the unpleasant feeling of guilt after you have done something you think is wrong.

controversial

A word used to describe an issue over which there is a great deal of disagreement. A controversial issue is often an issue about which the evidence and arguments are difficult to judge.

creationist

A creationist believes in creationism. Creationists believe that the Bible account of how the universe came about, that God created it in six days, is historically true. Creationists do not accept the theory of **evolution**, which claims that all modern-day species, including humans, have evolved slowly over time.

deduction

This is a **logical** way of **reasoning**. It involves making specific statements based upon general statements.

deductive

A way of **reasoning** by the use of **deduction**. It involves drawing **conclusions** that must, using **logic**, be necessarily true because they are based on broader true statements.

deism

The belief that there is a God but that God does nothing, or very little, to influence what goes on in the world.

deity

Another word for God. God is the more common word used in everyday speech where it is used virtually as a naming word for God. Deity is the less common word. It is used by thinkers and scholars, particularly when discussing what God is like.

divine

Another word for God. It is often used when talking about things that come from God, for example *a divine inspiration*. Also, it is used when talking about something that is like God.

divinity

A word used to describe something that comes from God. Sometimes it is used when talking about something, or someone, who has qualities that come from God.

dualism

The belief that there are two forces in the universe that are almost equal in power. One is a good force and the other is an evil force. Dualism is often seen as a belief in two gods, a good god and an evil god.

empirical

A way of gaining knowledge by relying on repeated experience and observation, supported by the **evidence** of our other senses.

empiricism

The belief that reasonable knowledge can be gained by using the **empirical** method. Empiricism claims that we can rely on knowledge if it is based on repeated experience, observation and careful experiment.

evidence

Evidence refers to the way in which something is thought to be true because there is good information or signs. Evidence does not provide an irrefutable proof. The word is often used to refer to information gained through one or more of the five senses: sight, sound, smell, touch or taste.

evolution

A theory made famous by Charles Darwin that claims that all forms of life alter (very slowly) over time by adapting to the environment. Evolution is often described as a challenge to the view that all life was created by God and since creation all animals and other forms of life have not changed at all.

generalising from the particular

Making a general claim based on a single example or a very limited number of examples. This usually results in an error, as a claim to knowledge is being made based on insufficient **evidence**. See also **anecdotal**.

hidden assumption

Often a person is unaware that they have made an **assumption**. When this happens, it is called a hidden assumption.

logic

A way of **reasoning**, which is thought to provide a conclusive and certain truth. Logic usually involves finding a first statement that is accepted as being true. Second and third statements can then be made which are also true as they necessarily arise out of the first statement.

logical

A way of thinking or presenting an argument that is based on **logic**. Being logical may describe what appears to be a very dry and formal argument. Or the word may describe an argument that is well reasoned, is clear and does not have any contradictions.

monotheism

The belief that there is only one God. For example, Islam, Christianity and Judaism are religions that believe in monotheism. Monotheism is a compound word as it is made up of two ancient Greek words: *mono*, which means 'one', and *theos*, which means 'god'.

moral

A word used when referring to almost anything to do with good or bad, whether it be thought or actions. The word can also be used when describing something that is good. For example, 'She was a very moral woman.'

myth

An imaginative story possibly containing a deeper message, which is often about God or human life. A myth may be open to different interpretations. Some people believe such stories are completely made up; some believe they are historically true; some that there might be a little bit of historical basis for them.

objective

Something that is clearly known to be true. Often it refers to knowledge that is claimed to be true, as it is not influenced in any way by human feelings, emotions or preferences.

omnipotence

A word meaning all-powerful. It is usually used to describe a characteristic of God. A God that is **omnipotent** is able to do everything; nothing is impossible for such a God. An omnipotent God has the power to do anything that God wants to do, is not limited by space or time but can be anywhere at any time, doing whatever it is that God chooses to do.

omnipotent

Having the power to do anything one wants to do. The word is usually used to describe a characteristic or quality of God (see **omnipotence**).

premise

A premise is a statement from which a true **conclusion** can be made. The word is used when talking about **logical reasoning**. Usually there must be two premises in order to make a logical conclusion.

psychoanalysis

Refers to a way of treating a person to improve their mental health. Based particularly upon the ideas of Sigmund Freud, psychoanalysis claims we repress memories. This can give rise to a sort of tension in the mind that can cause physical symptoms.

psychosomatic

The claim that a physical illness may be caused by the mind. A psychosomatic illness may appear to be a genuine physical illness but in fact the patient is suffering due to an illusion of their own making.

Qur'an

The holy book of Islam. Muslims believe the **Qur'an** was revealed to the Prophet Muhammad, and that it came directly from God.

reasoning

The attempt to provide a thought-through basis or motive for one's views or beliefs. Reasoning is usually associated with judgements based on sound principles, being consistent, identifying likely outcomes and making use of available **evidence**.

revelation

The claim that God continues to be active in the world after first creating it through things like visions, voices, messages and religious experiences. Revelation may be in the form of particular words, as in the belief that the holy book of Islam, the Qur'an, is a revelation from God.

sabr

An Arabic word used a lot in the **Qur'an**. It means putting up with problems with patience and fortitude. Sabr is a quality widely encouraged in Islam. A person with sabr would accept hardships in life without complaining or ever having doubts about God.

sceptic

A person who doubts or disbelieves. The word is often used to describe a person who believes that religious claims are unlikely. A sceptic may not say that religious beliefs are wrong but rather religion has uncertainties, which causes them to be very doubtful.

sceptical

The view held by a **sceptic**. Inclined to be critical and to have doubts, particularly about religious claims.

spiritual

A word often used to describe people who have an inner sense of well-being, derived from noble values or a sense of meaning to life. Also, often used to refer to the religious belief in an inner and higher self called the spirit.

subjective

Something it is hard to be sure is true. Often it refers to something that is in the mind of an individual rather than something that is real or is true outside of a person's mind. Something subjective may be the result of an emotion, feeling or personal preference, for example preferring chocolate to cake or enjoying hip hop more than easy listening.

surah

The **Qur'an** is divided into 114 sections, each of which is called a surah. Each surah is numbered to make it easier to find particular passages in the Qur'an.

theism

The belief that there is a God. Theism claims that God did not just sit back after creating the world but that God does things in the world. In particular, through **revelation**, God makes himself known.

theist

A person who believes that there is a God. A theist believes that God does things in the world, for example God makes himself known through revelation.

transcendent

Something that is outside of our normal experience or is beyond what we know using our five senses. Often the word is used when referring to a transcendent world. A transcendent world is claimed to be a higher world that exists but cannot be seen or touched.

Solution to crossword (p. 107)

Across

1. Surah 4. Myth 5. Logic 9. Morals 11. Evil 12. Plotinus 13. Premise 16. Atheist 17. Kant 18. Augustine 21. Sabr 23. Revelation 24. Cosmological

Down

2. Hume 3. Miracle 4. Mill 6. Omnipotent 7. Conscience 8. Paine 10. Good 11. Empiricism 14. Signs 15. Design 18. Analogy 19. Newman 20. Devil 22. Bacon

Acknowledgements

The author and publisher would like to thank the following for providing photographs:

Page 1/1 Archivo Iconografico/Corbis; 1/2 Photodisc 4 (NT); 3 Digital Vision 20 (NT); 7 Archivo Iconografico/Corbis; 8/1 Archivo Iconografico/Corbis; 8/2 Art Directors/Trip; 8/3 Bozi/Corbis; 8/4 Bettman/Corbis; 8/5 Topfoto; 8/6 Chris Hellier/Corbis; 11 Corel 133 (NT); 12 Corbis; 15 Bettman/Corbis; 16 Bettman/Corbis; 19/1 Corel 767 (NT); 19/2 Corel 795 (NT); 20 Corbis; 21a Photodisc 38B (NT); 21b Corel 795 (NT); 21c Corel 795 (NT); 21d Corel 658 (NT); 21e Gerry Ellis/Michael Durham/Digital Vision LC (NT); 21f Corel 126 (NT); 23/1 Michael Bisi/MEPL; 23/2 Largrellus and Westphal/MEPL; 23/3 Robbie Jack/Corbis; 23/4 Bettman/Corbis; 28 Rev Stuart Bell/Russels and Sons; 29 Bettman/Corbis; 30 Hulton Deutsch/Corbis; 31 Rick Friedman/Corbis; 32 Illustrated London News V1 (NT); 33/1 Archivo Iconografico/Corbis; 33/2 Art Directors/Trip; 34/1 Hulton Deutsch/Corbis; 34/2 Illustrated London News V1 (NT); 35/1 Corel 397 (NT); 35/2 Instant Art (NT); 35/3 Ingram ILP V2 CD6 (NT); 35/4 Corel 26 (NT); 37/1 Goldberg Diego/Corbis; 37/2 Corel 654 (NT); 37/3 Corel 654 (NT); 37/4 Alison Wright/Corbis; 37/5 Art Directors/Trip; 37/6 Leif Skoogfors/Corbis; 38 Bettman/Corbis; 39 Hulton Deutsch/Corbis; 40 MEPL; 41 Corel 75 (NT); 42/1 Bettman/Corbis; 42/2/3/4 Corel 75 (NT); 44 Corbis; 45 Fabian Cavellos/Corbis; 47/1 Bettman/Corbis; 47/2 Corel 640 (NT); 48 Corel 473 (NT); 49/1 Fabian Cavellos/Corbis; 49/2 Bettman/Corbis; 50/1 Illustrated London News V2 (NT); 50/2 Corel 647 (NT); 51/1 Photodisc 75 (NT); 51/2 Corel 759 (NT); 53/1 Francis G Mayer; 53/2 Photodisc 6 (NT); 54 Bettman/Corbis; 58/1 Digital Vision 9 (NT); 58/2 John Wesley Jarvis/Bettman/Corbis; 59 Corel 301 (NT); 62 Hulton Deutsch/Corbis; 63 Harald Theissen/Alamy; 64 Bettman/Corbis; 65/1 Francis G Mayer/Corbis; 65/3 Fabian Cavellos/Corbis; 66/1 Photodisc 6 (NT); 66/2 Photodisc 67 (NT); 69/1 Jim Reed/Digital Vision WW (NT); 69/2 Bettman/Corbis; 70/1 Corel 588 (NT); 70/2 Bettman/Corbis; 71 H Lips/MEPL; 72 Corel 495 (NT); 74 Stockbyte 28 (NT); 75/1Corel 723 (NT); 75b Corel 448 (NT); 76c Jim Reed/Digital Vision WW (NT); 76d Jim Reed/Digital Vision WW (NT); 76/3 Bettman/Corbis; 77 Francis G Mayer/Corbis; 78/1 Action Images/Corbis; 78/2 David Turnley/Corbis; 78/3 Helene Rogers/Alamy; 79/1 Corbis GS (NT); 79/2 Angel MEPL; 79/3 Corel 301 (NT); 81 Pearson/Bettman/Corbis; 82 MEPL/Alamy; 83 Archivo Iconografico/Corbis; 84 Rayoumont/MEPL; 85 Corel 304 (NT); 86 Photodisc 32 (NT); 87 Corel 707 (NT); 88MEPL; 89 Michael Nicholson/Corbis; 91/1 MEPL; 91/2 Archivo Iconografico; 92 Digital Stock 11 (NT); 93/1/2/3 Photodisc 16 (NT); 94 Photodisc 16 (NT); 96/1 SS/Fliegende Blatter/Harpers Weekly/Joseph Jastrow; 96/2 Swim Ink/Corbis; 97/1 Richard Swinburne; 97/2 Digital Vision 20 (NT); 99 Oldham Chronicle/Hulme Grammar School; 100/1 Robert Graves/MEPL; 100/2 Mikael Karlsson/Alamy; 100/2 Photodisc 71 (NT); 101 Photodisc 79 (NT); 102 Photodisc 5B (NT); 103 Photodisc 71 (NT); 104/1 Photodisc 4 (NT); 104/2 H Lips/MEPL; 105 Lebrecht/Alamy; 106 Photodisc 79 (NT); 108/1 Art Directors/Trip/Alamy; 108/2 Archivo Iconografico/Corbis; 108/3 Francis G Mayer/Corbis; 108/4 Bettman/Corbis; 109/1 Robert Graves/MEPL; 109/2 Bettman/Corbis; 109/3 Bettman/Corbis; 109/4 Oldham Chronicle/Hulme Grammar School; 110/1 Fabian Cavellos/Corbis; 110/2 Illustrated London News V1 (NT); 110/3 Hulton Deutsch/Corbis; 111/1 Bettman/Corbis; 111/2 MEPL; 111/3 Bettman/Corbis; 111/4 Archivo Iconografico/Corbis; 112/1 Bettman/Corbis; 112/2 Bettman/Corbis; 112/3 Hulton Deutsch/Corbis; 111/4 John Wesley Jarvis/Bettman/Corbis; 113/1 Corbis; 113/2 Rev Stuart Bell/Russels and Sons; 113/3 Bettman/Corbis; 114/1 H Lips/MEPL; 114/2 Corbis; 114/3 Bettman/Corbis; 114/4 Richard Swinburne; 114/5 Hulton Archive/Getty; 115/1 Archivo Iconografico/Corbis; 115/2 Rick Friedman/Corbis; 115/3 The Master and Fellows of Trinity College, Cambridge; 115/4 National Portrait Gallery/Jan Van Der Gucht/Bartholomew Dandridge; 115/5 Bettman/Corbis.

Picture research by Stuart Sweatmore.